Tae Kwon Do

TAE KWON DO

Dave Oliver

Text consultant: Dave Amerland

The Crowood Press

First published in 2002 by
The Crowood Press Ltd
Ramsbury, Marlborough
Wiltshire SN8 2HR

British Library Cataloguing-in-Publication Data
A catalogue record for this book is available from the British
Library.

ISBN 1 86126 454 2

Dedication
To my instructor, Bob Howe, who made the beginning possible,
and to Sue who made life complete. And I do not forget
Russell, Lucy, Michelle, Corin, Toby, Quentin, Cassie, Carly,
Dustin, Catherine, Shannon and Jamie who, each in their own
way, helped me make everything else happen. This book is for
you all.

The author and publisher cannot accept responsibility for
injuries or damage arising from the application of techniques
described in this book. It is recommended that you consult a
doctor before undertaking any physical activity.

Typeset by NBS Publications, Basingstoke, Hampshire

Printed and bound in Great Britain by J.W. Arrowsmith

Contents

Acknowledgements

It takes a lot of effort and hard work for any book to be born and this one is no exception. My thanks first and foremost must go to David Amerland for his ideas and excellent work on the script. I must thank everyone involved in Tae Kwon Do whom I have had the pleasure of meeting. Each, in their own way, helped produce the ideas which have gone into this book.

My thanks must go to 'the gang' who spent endless time going through all the requirements for the photographs used here and who carried them out again and again until they were perfect. Thanks also to Sylvio Dokov for his excellent photography.

Dave Oliver

The gang, from left to right.
Back row: Roger Lawrence, Dave Oliver, Tim Hobin.
Middle: Steve Merricks, Rebecca Brooks, Quentin Oury.
Front: Rebecca Riggs, Mark Shuter, Cassandra Oury.

Foreword

As a practitioner of Tae Kwon Do you will come across questions which at times may be difficult to ask. With this in mind, Dave Oliver (the United Kingdom's godfather of Tae Kwon Do), calling upon his thirty plus years' experience, has produced a book which can only be described as essential. It is said that 'the journey of enlightenment begins with a single step'. However, all travellers will arrive at their destination safer and quicker if they have an experienced guide to help them on their way. I suggest that you let this book be your guide – you will not be disappointed. You will have time to enjoy your journey and you will not get lost in the maze of mystery which surrounds the fantastic world of martial arts.

Paul Clifton
Editor of TKD-KMA *and* Combat *magazines*

The author.

Introduction

There are many reasons why you should take up Tae Kwon Do, and self-defence is only one of these reasons. Apart from the practical benefits of learning self-defence and improving your physical fitness, studying Tae Kwon Do will give you a window into the philosophy and traditions of a society that was old when Britain was still young.

Through the many events staged and hosted in the UK, you will be able to enjoy a wide circle of friends and contacts and become part of an ever-growing group of people for whom Tae Kwon Do has become more than just another sporting activity.

With its network of Tae Kwon Do clubs across the UK, the Tae Kwon Do Association of Great Britain (TAGB) is the main proponent of seminars, exhibitions and competitions which give you the opportunity to become involved in one of the liveliest of martial arts to a degree that suits your own personal aspirations and lifestyle.

Contrary to popular perception, you do not have to be young to begin Tae Kwon Do. Physical fitness, increased stamina, mental alertness and a serene state of mind are desirable attributes whatever stage of life you have reached, and with its adaptability in style Tae Kwon Do is uniquely suited to the many different needs of the individual in today's busy world.

I sincerely hope that picking up this book will be your first step into a journey that you will continue for the rest of your life.

The author with HRH Prince of Wales during a Tae Kwon Do demonstration.

1 State of the Art

Tae Kwon Do is a martial art which originated over twenty centuries ago in Korea. The earliest records of its practice date back to 50BC, where tomb paintings show men in fighting stances practising forms known as Taek Kyon.

It is believed that the origins of Taek Kyon date even further back and originated as self-defence against wild animals whose defensive and offensive movements were also the subject of much analysis. Taek Kyon at the time was only one style of fighting. Others had names such as Subak, Tak Kyon and so on.

By 57BC Korea had three kingdoms (Koguryo, Paekje and Silla) and, with a certain degree of inevitability, a strong rivalry between them led to a focus on the development of very effective fighting techniques.

History, repeatedly, has shown that it is the victor who writes the script and this case was no exception. Silla won its wars against its two rivals and in AD668 it unified the three kingdoms. Instrumental in its victory were the Hwa Rang Do, an elite group of young men who were devoted to cultivating their bodies and minds and serving the kingdom.

Hwa Rang Do, quite literally, means 'flowering youth' (Hwa = flower, Rang = young man) and the young noblemen of the Hwa Rang Do practised various forms of martial arts. The Hwa Rang Do also developed an honour code, and it is this which today forms the philosophical background of Tae Kwon Do.

In AD936 the Silla dynasty came to an end and with it the kingdom. In its place, Wang Kon founded the Koryo dynasty. Koryo is an abbreviation of Koguryo, which Wang Kon sought to revive. The modern name Korea is derived directly from the word Koryo.

It was during the Koryo that a new sport was given form. It was called Soo Bakh Do and it was used, principally, as a military training method. Drawing from the many different forms of martial arts which had preceded it, Soo Bakh Do used bare hands and feet as weapons. Its intensity was such that it was seen as a very good way of maintaining strength and overall fitness. As a result, its popularity spread throughout the kingdom of Koryo.

This was the precursor to modern day Tae Kwon Do. However, despite its effectiveness as a means of training for warfare and its popularity with the peasants in the fields, Soo Bakh Do went into decline after King Taejo, founder of the Yi dynasty, replaced Buddhism with Confucianism as the state religion. The teachings of Confucius, imported from the refined, rarefied culture of China, dictated that the higher class of man should read poetry and music and the practice of martial arts should be something left to the less refined, even inferior, man. By the end of the fifteenth century, Soo Bakh Do had almost disappeared.

The Yi dynasty lasted from 1392 to 1910 and during that time the practice of martial arts and the code of honour of the Hwa Rang remained alive in isolated, stubbornly traditional, cultural backwaters of Korea.

In 1910, Korea was invaded by Japan who dominated it until the end of World War II. The Japanese tried to erase all of the Korean culture, including its martial arts. As is usual with such situations, this brought a stubborn resurgence in the practice of martial arts which now, once more, had a very practical role to play against an invader who strictly controlled the supply of weapons.

Along with occupation, the Japanese also brought karate with them, and indeed the quick, straight-line movements which characterize many Tae Kwon Do moves today are a direct result of the legacy left behind by the Japanese army of occupation.

After the end of World War II, when Korea became independent, several Kwans, or fighting styles, arose. These were Chung Do Kwan, Moo Duk Kwan, Yun Moo Kwan, Chang Moo Kwan, Oh Do Kwan, Ji Do Kwan, Chi Do Kwan and Song Moo Kwan. All these Kwans were united in 1955 under the name of Tae Soo Do.

Korea's struggle to re-discover its identity and many traditions was, with some degree of inevitability, reflected in the subsequent development of its martial arts movement. By the beginning of 1957, several Korean martial arts masters had adopted the name Tae Kwon Do for their form of martial arts, because of its similarity to Tae Kyon.

The very first Tae Kwon Do students were soldiers, because General Choi Hong-Hi, who is credited as the father of modern Tae Kwon Do, required his soldiers to train in it. The police and air force were also required to train in Tae Kwon Do. At the time Tae Kwon Do was still very heavily under the influence of Japanese karate and, indeed, many of its moves and style bore a very close resemblance to Shotokan Karate.

In 1961, the Korean Tae Kwon Do Union arose from the Soo Bakh Do Association and the Tae Soo Do Association. In 1962 the Korean Amateur Sports Association acknowledged the Korean Tae Kwon Do Union and in 1965 it became the Korean Tae Kwon Do Association (KTA).

General Choi Hong-Hi, president of the KTA at the time, was asked to start the International Tae Kwon Do Federation (ITF) as the international branch of the KTA. What follows next is best described as the 'rise of the acronyms'. In 1961, following the overthrow of the southern government of Korea, General Choi left for Canada where he established the ITF as a separate entity in 1963. Tae Kwon Do was introduced into the UK in 1967, just four years after the foundation of the ITF.

Six years later, the World Tae Kwon Do Federation (WTF) was founded and in 1980 it was recognized by the International Olympic Committee (IOC) which made it a demonstration sport in the Olympic Games.

The Korea Tae Kwon Do Association (KTA) is the National Governing Body (NGB) for Tae Kwon Do in the Republic of Korea, just as the United States Tae Kwon Do Union (USTU) is the NGB for Tae Kwon Do in the United States. The World Tae Kwon Do Federation (WTF) is made up of Tae Kwon Do NGBs. These NGBs are member organizations of the WTF. Individuals can be affiliated to the WTF through their NGBs but cannot join the WTF directly.

As the popularity of Tae Kwon Do increased in the West, several attempts were made to unite the two Tae Kwon Do organizations. However, these were unsuccessful and in August 1983 it was decided to form, in the UK, an organization that would be run on principles far more democratic than were permitted by the two governing bodies of the time (the ITF and WTF). This became the basis of the Tae Kwon Do Association of Great Britain (TAGB).

Five years later, in April 1988, the TAGB became a founding member of the British Tae Kwon Do Council (BTC). The BTC is the only Tae Kwon Do body recognized by the United Kingdom Sports Council and it incorporates eleven different organizations.

The birth of the TAGB and the formation of the BTC represent a happy chapter in the tumultuous history of Tae Kwon Do. With the power of hindsight it is easy to make light of the differences between organizations that have more in common than not. It would, however, also be proper to reflect that the birth of Tae Kwon Do, its development and its propagation are as much a mirror of its troubled origin and the practical needs which made it possible as they are a telling remark on the apparent inability of its many governing bodies to cast aside their differences and find some common ground.

The TAGB, with over 18,000 members, represents the next stage in the development of Tae Kwon Do. With its grounding in the ethos and tenets which were first espoused by the Hwa Rang over 2,000 years ago and its open acceptance and constant development of new forms, training techniques and ideas, it stands poised to take an ancient fighting form into the twenty-first century, successfully linking the distant past with an equally distant, and certainly no less wondrous, future.

In view of this, in 1993, a new world body was formed called Tae Kwon Do International (TKDI). The new body encompasses both ITF and WTF stylists, is entirely non-political in orientation, and its sole aim is to promote worldwide the benefits of Tae Kwon Do as a sport and as a martial art. The TAGB is a founding member of this new body.

Tae Kwon Do is a sport for everyone. The benefits to young practitioners include better balance, increased speed and flexibility, and better overall fitness. All activities involving young Tae Kwon Do students are strictly supervised.

The self-defence side of Tae Kwon Do becomes apparent during
the practice of set routines which allow an individual to face one
or more attackers.

2　The First Step

Beginnings are never easy. The first step in any journey is fraught with the uncertainty of the unknown. Tae Kwon Do is no different, in that it can often give the impression that its practitioners, in common with those of other martial arts, exist in a self-enclosed, self-referential world which outsiders can enter only with difficulty.

Nothing could be further from the truth.

Since their inception all martial arts have been the most democratic of sports and fighting arts. Historically, they have been open to castes and classes of people whose station in life would have precluded them from most organized forms of sport.

This has been as true in China, Japan, Korea and the Philippines as it has been throughout the Western world. The reason martial arts are so outstandingly open to outsiders lies in the simple fact that they have traditionally been governed through meritocracy. In Tae Kwon Do, undoubtedly, you are always as good as your ability makes you, but what is more, you are always more equal than that.

But let us take things from the beginning and the beginning, invariably, has to be with the Tae Kwon Do training hall, or dojang.

A Night in the Dojang

Dojang means 'place of training in the way' and it is an acknowledgement that Tae Kwon Do is about more than just fighting.

Picking the Right Dojang

In a perfect world every Tae Kwon Do instructor would be affiliated to the organization that runs his or her type of Tae Kwon Do. Unfortunately this is not always the case. Clubs which do not belong to the organizing body of their brand of Tae Kwon Do are limited in the benefits that they can offer their students. Usually, their grades are not recognized outside the club as the validity of the grading system comes under suspicion. Do not be afraid to ask your instructor if he or she is a member of a national organization. If the answer is negative you should think carefully before deciding to join that particular dojang.

Traditionally dojangs were temples and there was a strict code of conduct for those who entered them. This was to avoid offending the gods as well as to show respect to all who trained there.

The modern dojang will be a purpose-built hall or a general-purpose room at a sports complex. When entering the students and the teacher show their commitment to the objectives of Tae Kwon Do by pausing at the door and performing a small bow. The student's bow, usually, is towards the teacher. If a teacher is not in the room at the time, a small bow is made to the senior student or performed towards the centre of the

A modern dojang is usually airy and well lit, with plenty of space for students to exercise in comfort and safety. If the dojang is a sports hall, the floor will usually be some suitable non-marking material. A bespoke dojang will have a sprung wooden floor or a carpet-covered floor with a 'soft' surface underneath. Suitable floor surfaces provide a safe environment for students to train in and minimize the stress and impact undergone by sensitive joints of the body such as the ankles and the knees.

room. The bow represents respect both towards the principles of Tae Kwon Do and those who train in it.

Once inside the dojang students are expected to behave with decorum. They must not smoke, talk loudly or eat and drink. When sitting they should rest with their backs against the wall and tuck their feet under them so that no one can trip over them.

At the beginning of training the teacher will call the class to order. The teacher stands at the front of the class and the students line up according to grade, with the senior students at the front and in parallel lines of descending grade.

Once the lines are correctly formed, the entire class comes to attention and bows to the teacher. The teacher then takes the class through a general warm-up routine in preparation for the training which is to follow. Occasionally, the teacher will ask senior students to take this warm up, in order to devote more time to moving around the class, closely observing students and helping them perfect their techniques. By allowing senior students to take warm ups or part of the lesson, the instructor also helps them to gain experience in conducting classes.

Tae Kwon Do training requires the repetition of techniques. Some of the techniques consist of very basic kicks, strikes, blocks or punches. Usually, the instructor will give a count and at each shout the class performs the technique in unison. Each time the instructor shouts, a single technique is performed. As it trains, the class gradually advances up the dojang until a natural limit is reached. The teacher then gives the command for a turn and the class performs it as one. As the lesson progresses, the basic techniques practised will begin to vary from line to line as the more advanced students are given more complex techniques to perform.

This compact form of training has a historical as well as a practical basis. Historically, unarmed martial arts has always been conducted clandestinely. It has been the preserve of the underclasses, who frequently laboured under the domination of a conqueror. The ability to be able to train in a relatively small space would, at that time, have been crucial in order to remain undetected by the enemy.

In practical terms, martial arts teach their practitioners control of their bodies. That means that an acute awareness of personal space and the ability to use it effectively must be developed as soon as possible. A class where students stand in straight lines next to each other while performing complex techniques is one of the quickest means of helping students to learn how to use a small space to their advantage without feeling claustrophobic or restricted in their moves in any way.

Repetition during practice is necessary in Tae Kwon Do because martial arts proficiency is gained when basic and even complex moves are 'hardwired' to the body and performed almost reflexively without the need to consciously think about them.

In the days when training in the martial arts was as necessary for survival as much as it was for fitness and peace of mind, it was not unusual for beginners to be given a single, basic technique, such as a punch or kick, to perform for weeks. Thankfully, these days this is no longer the case and the new student will very quickly be exposed to quite complex moves. Even so, part of each Tae Kwon Do lesson is devoted to repetition. This allows not only the building up of reflexes but also the development of better technique as students find ways to make their bodies perform more efficiently.

What happens after the basic techniques have been performed will depend largely upon the nature of the club and the inclination of the teacher. Almost always, the basic moves will give way to combination techniques which link two or more moves together and require the students to exercise balance, fluidity of movement and an awareness of the space they move in.

Clubs that have a good sparring record will pair students together for pair-form sparring or even free sparring. Both of these are practised under strict supervision and aim to teach students the concepts of distance and timing in attack and self-defence in a safe and yet challenging way. At some point in the lesson some form of physical conditioning will be carried out to improve strength, stamina or flexibility. These are all physical attributes that are useful in improving performance in Tae Kwon Do.

The lesson will finish with pre-arranged, stylized movements, called patterns, which are designed to help the student practise attack and defence moves against one or more imaginary attackers. These are executed to perfect form as well as improve co-ordination and balance.

Principles of Tae Kwon Do

Many clubs, these days, will offer the first lesson free to prospective students in the understanding that Tae Kwon Do is not necessarily for all, nor is everybody suited to Tae Kwon Do.

However, from the very first lesson prospective students will be made aware that training in Tae Kwon Do is more than just a means for becoming physically fitter and stronger. Bound within the traditions of the sport is the age-old belief that physical fitness is only a part of a larger whole, and to this end the student must endeavour to also attain moral, intellectual and psychological fitness.

There are five tenets governing the behaviour of Tae Kwon Do practitioners, which are: courtesy, integrity, perseverance, self-control and indomitable spirit.

Courtesy is extended by students not only to those above them whom they might naturally be expected to respect but also to all those below them in grade or ability.

Integrity lies in the willingness to be open and honest not only in dealings with others within the club but also, and arguably most importantly, with oneself.

Perseverance is the one quality no Tae Kwon Do practitioner can do without. In training, as in life, there are cycles. Sometimes things will go well, training techniques will fall together with a minimum of effort and rapid progression through the ranks will be made. At other times the going will be difficult, motivation will be low and the student will feel at a low point. It is at these times that anyone who trains in Tae Kwon Do will feel the need to look deep inside themselves in order to find the motivation needed to help continue training.

Self-control is vital. With proficiency in Tae Kwon Do comes a certain amount of power. Power, however, means little if it is not also bound by a sense of responsibility. The best Tae Kwon Do practitioners rarely feel the need to raise their voices in anger and never lose their tempers.

Indomitable spirit is the final tenet. It is a direct acknowledgement that there may come times in your life when the odds are truly stacked against you. This is the point at which most people would give up. It is here that Tae Kwon Do practitioners display their mettle by fighting their own uncertainty, conquering their fears and attaining the inner balance they need to find the confidence to continue.

All these are qualities which are equally suited to life outside the dojang as well as training within its walls, and for this reason Tae Kwon Do is often considered to be a way of life rather than just a martial art.

Something for Everyone

The great appeal of Tae Kwon Do is that it literally has something for everyone. There are two styles of Tae Kwon Do, which are recognized by their initials: TKDI (for Tae Kwon Do International) and WTF (for World Tae Kwon Do Federation). Apart from their separate governing bodies, their main difference lies in, for lack of a better word, their ideology in the way they approach physical contact in the sport. TKDI is a semi-contact sport. Hands and feet are covered by protective equipment and a headguard is worn at all times. Blows to the head can be delivered using either the hand or foot but they are controlled.

WTF (which is also the form of Tae Kwon Do represented in the Olympic Games) is a full-contact sport. Body armour is worn, along with a headguard. Punches to the head are not permitted, but kicks are. These differences become important when students start to consider competition sparring, but at an early level they will be relatively unimportant.

Because Tae Kwon Do is fast-moving and high-kicking it never becomes boring. The student can always find a goal to work towards. Whether it is flexibility, aerobic capacity, cardiovascular fitness, balance, strength or co-ordination, the horizon is constantly expanding.

All Kitted Out

Before joining a Tae Kwon Do club, a student will need to obtain the right equipment.

The first item required is a Tae Kwon Do uniform. This is uniformly white (except for black belt students who have a black trim). The uniform is comprised of a lightweight cotton top and equally lightweight cotton trousers. A belt is tied round the waist to signify the grade of the student. Unlike most other martial arts, which have a jacket style of top, the Tae Kwon Do top is smock-like. This prevents it from flapping open during exercise and competition sparring and it makes it easier for the student to maintain a neat appearance.

Apart from the uniform it is a good idea to invest in protective equipment. This, usually, is a legal requirement in order for students to be covered by the club's insurance against accidents, as well as a good, practical idea. Protective equipment consists of body armour (for WTF), hands and feet pads (for TKDI) and a headguard. A mouth guard is optional but usually a good idea. Male students will find that a groin guard is indispensable. Tae Kwon Do has rapid, high kicks and even with the best intentions in the world accidents can still

The Tae Kwon Do uniform consists of a lightweight cotton top and equally lightweight cotton trousers. The black belt uniform has an additional black trim along the collar. A different colour belt is worn to signify rank. Belts are tied in a particular way, and students usually will be shown how to tie their belts during the first lesson in which they wear their Tae Kwon Do uniform.

happen. The groin guards which work best are the ones worn by boxers, which have straps to keep them in place. Although they are not often called upon to protect that vital part of the male anatomy, when they are needed they are worth ten times their weight in gold!

Where Do We Go From Here?

Not long after that first lesson, most students will want to know how quickly they can grade, what the grading system is and who will be grading them. This is the first sign that already training in Tae Kwon Do has become more than just a fitness pursuit. Gradings indicate skill, competency and knowledge in Tae Kwon Do as well as

The Training Class

Tae Kwon Do is a sport for all. Although it is a 'hard' sport in the sense that it relies on muscular strength and fitness for effectiveness, rather than the inner energy (or chi) of martial arts like Aikido, it can still help 'weaker' practitioners triumph over stronger ones through the application of superior strategy, clearer thinking and faster execution of techniques. To this extent men and women train together and often spar against each other. This helps both sexes, as each is forced to adapt to the style and way of fighting of the other.

physical ability, and form a journey in their own right.

3   Fly Like a Butterfly

Every martial art has a grading system of some description, and Tae Kwon Do is no exception. Grading is necessary in order to establish a structured progression in the student's development in Tae Kwon Do. Without a properly supervised grading system, a martial art descends into anarchy where the only recognition lies in just how hard individuals can kick or punch and how physically fit they are.

Martial arts in general, and Tae Kwon Do in particular, are more than just that. Progress means that students become not just fitter at a physical level but also more knowledgeable. They acquire the psychological and mental toughness to complement their physical ability and, in the process, further develop their personal set of values.

While this may sound like a tall order for what, at times, is nothing more than a hobby for Western students, it is also the fundamental difference between martial arts and any other kind of sport.

Progress is linked to the development of students' inner resources as well as physical ability and the grading system is necessary as an indicative measure of the development of both.

The Grading System

Tae Kwon Do uses a coloured belt system. There are six colours of belts, but twelve steps between the level of the beginner student (signified by the white belt) and that of the advanced student (signified by the black belt). The twelve steps are created through the use of what are known as 'half belts'. The student who attains a half belt has reached an interim level of skill and ability approximately half-way between two full belts.

The reason that there are twelve steps as opposed to six is to give the student the opportunity to advance at a pace which is more suited to the busy Western lifestyle. It is also helps students to advance from one level of competency to the next, as at the half-belt level they can more easily prepare themselves and acquire the knowledge and develop the skills which will be required of them in order to reach the next belt.

Every student entering Tae Kwon Do for the first time starts off from the white belt. Progression up the ladder towards the black belt depends upon a variety of factors: how quickly a student develops in ability, frequency of training, physical fitness and personal aptitude.

In keeping with the wider, overall philosophy of Tae Kwon Do, the six colour belts signify something deeper than just a certain degree of skill.

White: signifies innocence. The innocence of the beginning student who has no knowledge of Tae Kwon Do.

Yellow: signifies the earth from which a plant sprouts and takes root as Tae Kwon Do foundations are being laid.

Green: signifies the plant's growth as training in Tae Kwon Do continues and the student's skills develop.

Blue: signifies the heaven towards which the plant matures into a towering tree as training in Tae Kwon Do progresses.

Red: signifies danger, cautioning the student to exercise control and warning the opponent to stay away.

Black: is the opposite to white. It therefore completes the circle and signifies the maturity and proficiency in Tae Kwon Do that the student has attained. It also signifies the wearer's imperviousness to darkness and fear.

Gradings are events which, depending on the number of students attending, can last anything up to three hours. Belts in Tae Kwon Do indicate that a student has reached a particular level of skill in the execution of Tae Kwon Do techniques and has, in the process, attained a certain degree of knowledge.

As such it does not automatically imply that a black belt student will be able to automatically defeat in sparring a red belt student. Proficiency in sparring is the direct result of time invested in training, talent and aptitude and as such forms only a small part of Tae Kwon Do. The belt system, and the gradings, take this into account. Students are examined for correct execution of techniques, and are tested for their understanding and knowledge of the system that they train in.

A black belt student may not automatically be the best fighter in the dojang but he or she will always be the most knowledgeable, able to give guidance and advice on the correct execution of techniques to all those belts below him or her.

Rules and Regulations

Because Tae Kwon Do techniques are potentially lethal, rules are necessary to ensure the safety of all practitioners. The rules state that

The spectacular head-high kicks of Tae Kwon Do are the result of flexibility work and dynamic stretching in class. Accuracy in kicking is every bit as important as power. To help students achieve accuracy instructors often use focus pads which give them a target for their kicks. Good kicks are the result of application rather than talent. The repetition work done in the dojang helps students develop the strength, speed and muscular co-ordination necessary for such kicks.

in training as well as in competition, sparring kicks to the lower body (including the groin

Age, sex, height and individual physical characteristics are no barrier to success in Tae Kwon Do. The training is always focused to allow individuals to make the most of their best physical attributes while developing better athletic ability. The emphasis, always, is on safety, with students advancing in a carefully structured way that will take them through the ranks all the way to the coveted black belt level.

area), sweeps and ground fighting are strictly prohibited. The back, neck and throat areas are also not regarded as targets. That leaves the body from the waist to the collarbone and the head as the only acceptable targets.

In semi-contact Tae Kwon Do (TKDI) the head can be punched as well as kicked, though blows are always controlled rather than full force. In full-contact Tae Kwon Do (WTF) the head is a valid target for kicks only and cannot be punched. As a general rule of thumb, kicks to the head in WTF tend to be harder than in TKDI.

Competitions

Tae Kwon Do will give a student the opportunity to participate in competitions and competition sparring. At any one time, all over the world, tens of thousands of men, women and children take part in Tae Kwon Do competitions. These range from local competitions organized between clubs, to regional and national competitions which culminate with the annual World Tae Kwon Do competitions.

A student can start competing at any belt, and will usually be matched with people of a similar weight and level of skill (children are matched by age and height as well as belt level). As success in competition sparring requires practice and experience, the more competitions that you enter, the faster you will gain the experience necessary and improve your own performance.

Competitions are always expertly refereed and supervised. Everyone taking part has to have the mandatory protective equipment and contact, even in the full-contact events, is kept to an acceptable level, the aim being to showcase skill and speed in the execution of techniques rather than brute force.

Competition sparring is an exciting, fun and safe aspect of Tae Kwon Do but, although a large number of men, women and children take part in these competitions, they still form only a small proportion of the overall number of people who are active practitioners of Tae Kwon Do.

Some students prefer to take part in competitions but enter only the breaking events or the patterns. Others go only for the sparring, while others still choose to go for all three. The choice is a personal matter, depending largely on preferences and circumstances. The aim, as always, is to enjoy the chosen option, otherwise it becomes a chore. Competitions, whether in sparring, patterns or breaking, help to focus the mind and help the Tae Kwon Do practitioner to pull together all the disparate elements which go into making Tae Kwon Do such an exciting, demanding and addictive martial art.

Some students claim that competitions help them to speed up the development of their inner resources. Others like to take part in competitions because the preparation entails a lot of physical training. However, everyone who takes part highlights the fact that training in Tae Kwon Do is beneficial at more than just a physical level. There are mental and psychological benefits to be derived and, in their entirety, these form a complete training package from which everybody can benefit irrespective of age, sex or personal level of physical fitness.

Physical Benefits

Tae Kwon Do is what is normally described as a 'hard' type of martial art. This means that physical fitness is an integral part of every lesson. With its fast moves and high kicks Tae Kwon Do helps develop stamina; strength; speed; aerobic capacity (how effectively oxygen is used in the lungs and taken to the muscle groups and organs in the body which need it the

Every Little Helps

Physical fitness is probably one of the hardest things to maintain in today's stress-ridden, fast way of life. Many people make resolutions about fitness which they never keep because they think that it would require more time and effort than they have available to give. Physical fitness is a cumulative effect. Ten minutes spent doing sit-ups and press-ups each night, for example, by the end of the working week has added up to almost an hour of exercise which otherwise would not have taken place. The hardest thing, perhaps, is not to formulate a training routine but to stick to it. The trick is to keep it simple and to aim low. For example, a daily routine of five to ten minutes of exercise is easier to maintain long term than a twenty-minute workout. Also, it is helpful to choose activities that require neither a lot of space nor complicated equipment. Aim to do exercises that can be done at home first thing in the morning, before you hit the shower or last thing at night before you go to bed. Then sit back and reap the benefits.

most); cardiovascular fitness (how quickly muscle groups and the body's major organs are fed nutrients by the blood and have their waste by-products removed); and flexibility.

Each Tae Kwon Do lesson is structured in such way that most if not all of these elements will be included. In addition many students find it beneficial to supplement their training routine with running, jogging, squash or some other aerobically demanding form of training.

What extra training is necessary is entirely a matter of personal choice. Female students and children are naturally more flexible and may not need to do extra work on their flexibility. Men, depending on their body type, might typically have to work on speed, aerobic capacity, flexibility or even strength.

Some practitioners find that the lessons are enough for their needs and they need to do very little or no extra work. What is important is that by addressing all these aspects of physical fitness Tae Kwon Do becomes a very rounded means of getting fit and maintaining that fitness.

Increased strength and endurance and a better muscle tone are a direct benefit all practitioners start to enjoy within the first few weeks of joining. Because of the physically demanding lessons they also find that it is much easier to control their weight than before they started training.

The physical aspect, however, is only one part of Tae Kwon Do training. Of equal importance are the mental and psychological benefits to be had.

Men, generally, have to work harder on flexibility of the tendons to allow them to do kicks like this, while women and children, who are naturally more flexible, have to improve on their speed and strength.

The Mental Angle

Physiological studies have shown that a minimum of twenty minutes of vigorous exercise once a week increases the blood flow delivered by the heart to the brain and helps maintain mental sharpness and even a higher IQ.

Most Tae Kwon Do lessons last a minimum of one hour and are carried out two or three times a week. Practitioners feel mentally more alert and this has very positive results in their outlook on life as well as their general well being.

The ancient Greek adage of 'A sound mind in a sound body' is a principle inherent in all aspects of Tae Kwon Do.

Feeling Good

Being fit and mentally alert has a direct impact on the psychology of the individual.

Tae Kwon Do practitioners are psychologically more confident in themselves and their own abilities. Many adopt the guiding tenets of Tae Kwon Do as a personal code of conduct outside the dojang as well as inside it.

Feeling good about yourself is an important part of the personal bio-feedback cycle. People who feel good are more likely to make the right decisions in their lives, and less likely to be affected by stress at work. They are also less prone to illnesses such as the common cold and are more resistant to fatigue and exhaustion.

By now of course you will have realized that Tae Kwon Do is a means, not an end. Like life, it is a journey of self-discovery where all practitioners, sooner or later, will come up against their own doubts, fears and limitations and will have to recognize them and defeat them in order to progress.

This is the personal, private almost, side of Tae Kwon Do. It is what goes on inside the heart and mind of each man, woman and child who enters a dojang. However, this life-enhancing inward journey begins from the physical side of Tae Kwon Do.

4   The Perfect Stance

It was Bruce Lee who, in an open lecture on martial arts, once said that 'the perfect martial artist is one who makes his fighting stance his normal day stance and his normal day stance his fighting stance'. What he meant by those words was not, as has sometimes been assumed, that you should go through life constantly on the alert for trouble which may never appear, but that there should be no difference between a martial arts fighting stance and the way in which you walk and stand each day when they are examined from the perspective of harmony and balance.

There are many stances in Tae Kwon Do and a certain amount of debate has gone into their importance. It has been pointed out, in the past, that during competition sparring the most effective moves usually come out of stances that fall outside the formal requirements of dojang training. It has also been said, quite correctly, that self-defence takes no stances into account for its execution.

All this raises the question of why the stances are needed at all. Why so many? What role do they serve?

Balance, Strength and Harmony

In 1997 the British paratroop regiment, reputedly with some of the toughest and most physically rugged men in the world in its ranks, carried out an interesting test with the help of the British Army's physiomedical unit.

They were in the Sudan, where the local women habitually carry as much as eight stone (50kg) of weight in water and local produce in big baskets which they carry on their heads as they walk the 2 miles (5km) from their village to the market and back. The baskets are balanced on thick rope or vine rings which act as a cushion and the women do this walk daily in heat as high as 36°C without showing any outward signs of fatigue.

The army doctors wired the local women and a group of volunteers from the paratroop regiment to monitoring equipment that measured the muscle tension and worked out the effort expanded and the number of calories being used. To their surprise, the local Sudanese women used no extra calories at all getting their loads to the market and back. The superbly fit paratroopers, on the other hand, used tremendous amounts of energy in order to complete the task and, at the end of it, showed signs of fatigue.

The reason for this lies in the fact that the paratroopers were attempting to do the task without having being 'taught' to do so and were thus being forced to use their physical strength and stamina to achieve it. In contrast, the village women of the Sudan have to carry such loads from a very young age and have learnt to walk in such manner that the weight of the load is carried by their skeletons rather than by the muscles of their bodies.

They are, in other words, in balance.

They move in harmony and because of this they exhibit strength which is seemingly unnatural to their build and general physique.

This is exactly the role played by stances in martial arts. They are teaching aids, developed over thousands of years to aid in the development of the type of balance that leads to harmonious movements. A balanced, harmonized body does not fight with its own weight and can thus perform to its optimum ability giving results that most untrained people, even if they are physically fit, can only dream of.

Stances in Tae Kwon Do play a vitally important role in overall fitness and performance and it is always a good idea for the beginner as well as for the advanced student to practise them at every opportunity.

They are also useful training aids when there is not much time, a lot of room or the equipment to exercise. A stance held for any length of time trains many of the muscles of the body that are used in the correct execution of Tae Kwon Do techniques.

The Stances of Tae Kwon Do

Ready Stance (Also Known as Parallel Ready Stance)

Stand with your feet about shoulder-width apart, toes pointing to the front. Shoulders are held square, body erect, but relaxed. Hands are held in a light fist to the front with the elbows slightly bent. This is a perfect balance stance. There is no muscle of the body here which is too relaxed or too tense. This is the preparatory stance (as the name suggests) for springing into action. In class it is the stance used most often between the execution of techniques. It is also the stance the student most often returns to when in line.

When students stand at attention in class, they hold their hands by their sides, feet together and pointing forward. Standing at the ready, feet are about a shoulder-width apart, toes still pointing to the front. The arms are now held to the front of the body, elbows slightly bent, fists lightly clenched. The body is held straight but relaxed. In this stance the student is ready to spring into action.

Sitting Stance

Stand with legs about double shoulder-width apart with toes facing towards the front. Knees are bent at what is an almost 90 degree angle. The weight of the body is evenly distributed on each leg and the trunk is held upright so that the centre of gravity is directly over the hips. The sitting stance is very good for developing strong leg muscles. It also helps to develop a low centre of gravity. This is particularly useful when it comes to developing throwing techniques, which are part of the student's personal self-defence arsenal but not part of official Tae Kwon Do teaching. This stance is particularly useful for the development of good, strong, kicks.

Walking Stance

As the name suggests this is a stance used in class in a forward and backward motion when practising repetitive sets of techniques. The front foot is about double the shoulder-width away from the back foot. Both feet are turned so that the toes face towards the front. The knee of the front leg is bent to about 60 degrees. The knee of the back leg is perfectly straight. The weight of the body is evenly distributed between the front and back legs and the centre of gravity is directly over the hips. The trunk is held straight and upright.

This stance exercises the strength of the legs as they hold the weight of the body. It also helps develop flexibility in the calves.

Sitting stance.

Walking stance.

Tight calf muscles slow movement down and often cause injury in the hamstrings (back of the thighs). The walking stance is also a stance that can be used in training to aid in the development of awareness regarding the importance of mobility and balance and the trade off between the two. Bend your front knee more, make your stance wider and you become less mobile but harder to push off your feet. Make the stance narrower, bring your feet closer together and you can move around faster but you can be caught off balance by a sudden lunge push and thrown off your feet.

L-Stance

This is often thought of as the classic Tae Kwon Do stance because so many Tae Kwon

L-stance.

The Power of the L-Stance

Nothing in Tae Kwon Do is done accidentally. Everything has come about as a result of trial and error over thousands of years in often perilous situations and the L-stance is no exception. Every vital part of the body is to be found upon an imaginary line drawn from the top of your forehead, just above your eyes, to your groin. The human body has been designed to fight in a forward position (hence our bifocal vision) but to do so in a hostile situation also means exposing the nose, throat, heart, sternum, solar plexus and groin to potentially damaging blows. The alternative is the L-stance. By turning the body sideways, it allows you to fight in a forward position without exposing some of the body's most vulnerable points to direct attack. By limiting the number of targets available, this stance also limits the possible forms of attack which can be launched (particularly in competition sparring, where the back and lower parts of the body are not valid targets and cannot be attacked).

Do practitioners adopt it as their sparring stance. In the L-stance both knees are bent. The front foot points to the front. The back foot is placed about a shoulder-width and a half behind it, in direct line with it and turned at 90 degrees to the body. The stance derives its name from the fact that if an imaginary line were drawn from the back of the heel of the front foot to the back of the heel of the back foot and then through the toes it would form a perfect 'L' shape.

In the L-stance the centre of gravity is again over the hips but the weight distribution is split on a 60:40 basis. Sixty per cent of the weight is on the back leg and only 40 per cent is on the front. For someone new to Tae Kwon Do, the L-stance feels awkward and 'alien' but it is, however, one of the best stances possible in terms of versatility and probably one of the few which will work in a fighting situation outside the dojang.

Fixed Stance

This is an older, more stylized but nevertheless very useful stance. It is formed exactly like the L-stance but this time the weight distribution of the body is divided equally between the front and the back leg. This makes it less mobile than the L-stance, but it is a structurally stronger stance which has many uses.

Fixed stance.

Vertical Stance

This stance is based on the L-stance. The knees are straight and the distance between the heel of the front foot and the heel of the back foot is zero. The body is held perfectly straight and the weight distribution, inevitably in a standing stance like this, is 50:50.

Bending Stance

Of all the stances this perhaps is the least stable. It requires strong legs and trunk and a perfect sense of balance to execute. This is a one-legged stance with the supporting leg, as the name suggests, slightly bent! That leg takes the body's entire weight. The other leg is bent at the knee and drawn up so that the flat of the foot is held near the kneecap of the

Bending stance.

supporting leg. The trunk is held upright and the centre of gravity, for such a seemingly precarious stance, is as close to the centre of the hips as possible.

There are many practical uses for a stance like this in a martial art famed for its kicks. From this position a number of different kicks can be delivered to what can be devastating effect. In practice it is highly unlikely that a stance like this will be required to be held for anything more than a few seconds. Being able to hold this stance however, teaches tremendous control over the muscles of the body. Inevitably, awareness of balance and, yes, harmony, are required in order to be able to hold this stance for anything longer than thirty seconds.

X-Stance

This is an almost vertical stance in the sense that the knees are only lightly bent. The back leg crosses behind the front one to get to the front by about the width of the closed fist. Most of the weight for this stance and, indeed, most of the stabilizing role, is taken by the 'back' leg which is balanced on the ball of the foot.

Rear Foot Stance

This stance is exactly what it says it is and it also illustrates the propensity of Tae Kwon Do stances to be named after the foot which is taking most of the body's weight and is doing most of the hard work. The rear foot stance is like the L-stance. Once again, 60 per cent of the body's weight is supported by the back leg while 40 per cent is supported by the front. The front leg rests on the ball of the foot. Both knees are bent. The distance between them would be the width of a closed fist if the heel of the front leg were allowed to touch down.

Rear foot stance.

Low Stance

This is identical in structure to the walking stance only this time the distance between the front foot and the back foot is exaggerated by another half a shoulder width at least.

This is a stance that dates back to the very roots of Tae Kwon Do and was used as a training stance to strengthen the muscles of the legs for kicking. Training any length of time in a low stance is an energy-intensive form of training which also promotes endurance, which is perhaps another reason it was used.

Fist.

The Ultimate Weapon

All these stances, of course, would be of no use whatsoever if the instrument they were designed to aid was not itself one of the most adaptable, versatile and deadly ones in the world.

Lacking claws, scales, poisonous toxins, or long sharp teeth, and suffering, for lack of a better word, from a muscle type which wastes away when it is not used (unlike our animal cousins), the human body neverthe-less manages to display a sophisticated armoury of weapons.

The trick, however, is to know exactly which weapon to apply to what target.

Fist

Hard bone, particularly on the two front knuckles. Effective for delivering fast, deci-sive blows. Particularly useful for attacking areas such as chin, nose and mouth and soft parts of the body such as the solar plexus, kidneys and spleen.

Fingers

Hard to deflect but easy to damage if used against a hard target. The fingertips are par-ticularly useful for attacking such soft targets as the solar plexus, the throat and the eyes. Fingers have no muscle. They are all ten-don so they cannot be flexed. To 'stiffen'

Fingers.

them and protect them against damage it is customary to hold them bent a little so they all present a unified edge with the tips of the first three fingers being at the same height.

The Heel of the Palm

The heel of the palm is a part of the body known as naturally hard. It has practically

The heel of the palm.

solar plexus, the kidneys, the sternum and the clavicles (in a downward linear motion).

The Edge of the Palm

The edge of the palm is also what is known as a 'natural weapon' in that, like the palm heel and the elbow, it has few major nerves running through it. Unlike the other two, however, it is a mass of soft tissue and has no thick, hard bone in it. As such the edge of the palm is effective only against relatively

no major nerves. As such it feels little pain and there is precious little soft tissue to damage when striking something hard. The palm heel is useful for delivering devastatingly powerful blows to such areas as the nose (which is potentially lethal), the chin and even the solar plexus.

Elbow

The elbow also forms a naturally hard area of the body. The elbow joint itself is very well protected and the bones forming it are amongst the hardest in the body. Because of its location, the elbow is not very well suited to an attack to the front of the body. To use it we have to either angle our bodies to the side (for a linear movement) or choose a curved motion and bring it to bear to the front. Furthermore, because elbow attacks out of necessity require that the forearm is bent and held back, it is a weapon best used at close quarters.

It is very well suited for attacks to the side and behind and its power is attested to by the fact that it is so often used as the technique of choice for breaking through boards. Areas of the body which can very successfully be attacked using elbow strikes are the temple,

The edge of the palm.

The Famous Martial Arts 'Chop'

The so-called 'karate chop' is probably one of the most enduring film images of martial arts. This time there is a certain degree of truth behind the hype. It is possible to condition the edge of the palm so that a thick, protective layer of hard skin forms. Because the hands can move so fast, delivering a blow with the edge of the palm can be very effective because it concentrates a lot of power onto what is relatively a small surface area. This makes breaking boards possible as well as damaging much softer targets such as the human body.

soft targets such as the back of the neck, the side of the neck and the throat. Paradoxically the edge of the palm can be conditioned through repetitive use to form a hard, calloused surface which then makes it an almost ideal weapon. Martial arts films have embedded the image of the martial artist using nothing but the edge of the palm to cut through thick pieces of wood, like a cleaver, or chop down opponents.

Knee

The kneecap forms a hard, natural protection for the sensitive joint of the knee, which is designed to absorb hard impacts. As such, it makes a perfect weapon against targets such as the groin, the solar plexus and (from a sideways impact) the knee joint itself.

Instep

The instep of the foot is a relatively wide area and although it is the first area of attack which presents itself on the foot, it is the equivalent of using the open hand to slap.

Furthermore there are a lot of small bones in the instep which are quite fragile. To use it to attack a hard target like a shin, knee, or elbow is to invite disaster as broken bones in the instep are particularly painful. The instep is best used to attack soft areas of the body like the groin, or areas where a large bundle of nerves is very close to the surface of the skin, like the face.

The Ball of the Foot

At first glance this is not a very obvious weapon. Yet the ball of the foot is the equivalent of the two front knuckles in the fist. It is relatively hard, not very sensitive to pain (unless you happen to kick something sharp and very hard) and it is able to deliver a powerful blow (powered by the whole strength and speed of the leg, no less) to a small, concentrated area thereby increasing its effectiveness severalfold. Delivered by someone who knows what he or she is doing, a ball of the foot kick is very difficult to stop. Areas of attack are the solar plexus, the groin, the knees and any major muscle group (which will cramp).

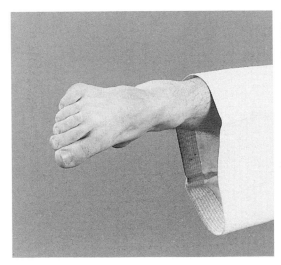

Instep.

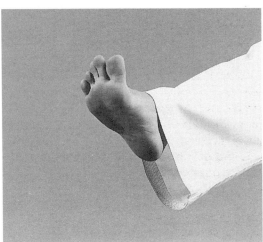

The ball of the foot.

The Heel

Like its counterpart in the hand, the heel of the foot is a naturally hardened area of the body. It can be used in a straight line attack (like in a back kick) or a vertical attack from above (like in an axe kick). There is one slight problem. In the hand the muscles of the arm cannot generate sufficient power to damage the palm heel. The leg muscles, however, are a different story. Too hard a kick against the wrong target will cause the bone of the heel to rupture its protective sheath and cut into the flesh of the foot from the inside, rendering walking difficult. The heel is best used as a devastating weapon against soft targets such as the solar plexus and groin. A properly hardened heel, however, can make for spectacular back kick breaks using wooden boards.

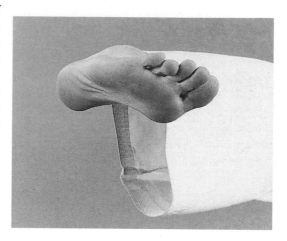

The edge of the foot.

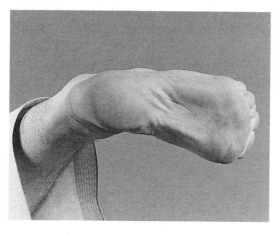

The heel.

The Edge of the Foot

The edge of the foot (also known as the foot sword) seems one of the most unlikely weapons. For a start the foot has to be angled in order for it to be presented. Secondly, it seems effective only on linear attacks (kicks in a straight line). Thirdly, although some toughening can be achieved there does not seem to be a substantial enough area presented to work on. And yet the edge of the foot is a superb weapon. It is used almost exclusively in the side kick. By angling the foot to present the side all the delicate bones of the foot are removed from harm's way. The edge of the foot is narrow, with a high pain threshold and, when powered by the entire strength of the leg, capable of breaking through three and four one inch boards! Used against any of the soft or hard targets of the body (even the head) it is a potent weapon.

Other Natural Weapons

Although only those parts of the body which martial arts teaches for use as weapons within the dojang are discussed here, of course there are other natural weapons, such as the nails, teeth and forehead. These are more suited to a streetfight situation, and although a martial artist who by the unluckiest of circumstances is involved in a confrontation may need to use every available means of defence, it is to be hoped that those who study a martial art would be unlikely to find themselves in such situations. Awareness of potential danger is a skill which can be developed and which will help to keep you out of trouble.

Vulnerable Points

Having seen the vast potential of the body as a weapon, it is only natural to now examine the parts of it which are possible targets.

In competition sparring and normal Tae Kwon Do training the target areas are the upper body from the waist upwards (but not the back) and the head. Contact is strictly controlled and practitioners are always well protected with pads and headguards. What is more, fighting is organized around a points system where points are scored depending on which part of the body has been targeted. This helps focus on the execution of Tae Kwon Do techniques, and eliminates the need for the application of brute force.

Tae Kwon Do, however, dates back to a time when fighting ability was closely linked to survival and contact went decidedly beyond the gentlemanly atmosphere of the dojang and, as such, it was designed to inflict serious damage.

To achieve this its practitioners studied the human body closely to uncover its vulnerable points. The body is, traditionally, divided into three distinct areas, each of which has points that can be utilized by the adept martial artist to gain the most advantage out of an attack. The three areas are high, middle and low section.

The High Section

- **Top of the head**: the skull is weak where the frontal and parietal bones join. A forceful blow (from an axe kick for example) causes trauma to the cranial nerves, resulting in unconsciousness

and vascular shock. A particularly sharp blow could cause death.

- **Forehead**: a forceful blow could cause whiplash injury from the sudden change in head position. A very sharp blow causes concussion.
- **Temples**: the bone structure of the skull is very weak at this point and the meningeal artery and a large nerve lie close to the skin surface. A powerful blow causes unconsciousness and concussion of the brain. A sharp blow might shatter the bone structure and pinch the meningeal artery.
- **Eye**: a slight poke in this area causes uncontrollable watering of the eyes, blurred vision and even temporary blindness. A forceful blow will rupture the eyeball causing permanent blindness.
- **Ear**: a blow to the ear can burst the eardrum and may cause nerve shock or internal bleeding.
- **Nose**: the nose is composed of thin cartilage material and has many blood vessels close to the surface. A blow can break the cartilage causing extreme pain and eye-watering blindness. A very sharp blow can cause unconsciousness through the overload of pain. A powerful blow delivered with a large surface area at right angles to the nose (like a palm heel for example) will cause the bones forming the bridge of the nose to break up and fragment, driving bone splinters upwards into the brain and causing instant death.
- **Upper lip**: the area immediately under the nose has several very sensitive nerves running just under the surface of the skin. A sharp blow causes unconsciousness and possible concussion. A lesser blow brings intense pain and a lot of eye-watering blindness. It also can chip or loosen teeth.

- **Jaw**: a hard blow to the jaw could fracture it or dislocate it from its hinge. If the facial nerve is pinched against the edge of the lower jaw one side of the face will be paralysed.
- **Chin**: the chin is the traditional target in boxing. The jaw acts as a lever which relays the force of the blow to the back of the head, to the medulla. As the medulla controls the cardio-respiratory mechanism a powerful blow to the jaw induces unconsciousness and concussion.
- **Throat**: a blow to the throat will sever or constrict the windpipe causing serious damage which can easily lead to death. A lesser blow is extremely painful and will cause gagging, choking and vomiting.
- **Side of the neck**: a sharp blow to the side of the neck will cause unconsciousness by shock, produced when the jugular vein, the carotid artery and the vagus nerve which run along the side of the neck, under the skin, are struck.
- **Back of neck**: whiplash, concussion, a broken neck and death will result from a blow to this area.

The Middle Section
The middle section includes the entire region of the body below the shoulders and above the hips.

- **Collar bone**: the collar bone breaks at about 8lb (3.6kg) of pressure applied at right angles to it. It disables an opponent's arm and causes extreme pain.
- **Armpit**: a large bundle of nerves lie close to the skin under each armpit. A blow here causes severe pain and temporary partial paralysis.
- **Spine**: the spinal column houses the spinal cord and a blow can dislocate the column resulting in paralysis or death.
- **Heart**: sometimes a jolting blow to the heart is used to set up a knockout blow somewhere else. A sufficiently powerful blow will make the heart suffer from temporary arythmia.
- **Solar plexus**: this is another target favoured by professional boxers. It is a large collection of nerve cells which forms the centre of the sympathetic nervous system. Blows to this area are very painful. A really powerful blow will induce a shock strong enough to cause unconsciousness.
- **Diaphragm**: a blow near the lower frontal ribs will severely wind an opponent. A hard blow will relax the diaphragm and intercostal muscles, forcing the air out of the lungs and stopping all breathing until they are ready again to expand and contract.
- **Spleen**: the spleen is located inside the lower rib cage on the left side and just beside the kidney. A powerful blow from the front or the side can rupture the spleen.
- **Elbow**: the elbow joint is a particularly vulnerable part of the body because when it is held straight and struck against its bending angle it requires only about 15lb (7kg) of pressure to break.
- **Wrist**: the wrist is another joint which is easy to break when struck correctly.
- **Fingers**: the fingers are always susceptible to sprains and breaks, particularly if the opponent is not careful about how they are held.
- **Kidneys**: certain large nerves branching off from the spine are close to the surface over the kidneys. A powerful blow can rupture the kidney causing severe nervous shock or death.

The Low Section

The low section includes the entire region of the body below the hips.

- **Bladder**: a powerful blow to this area could rupture the bladder. A really penetrating blow could fracture the pubic bone and puncture the colon.
- **Groin**: any blow, even a slight one, to this area causes extreme pain for men. Pain, shock, loss of breath, vomiting and even unconsciousness are commonly associated with really powerful blows to this area.
- **Coccyx**: a really hard blow to this target will fracture the bone and cause severe pain.
- **Knee**: the kneecap takes about 70lb (32kg) of pressure to dislocate. A hard kick to this joint will tear ligaments and cartilage and cause extreme pain. A powerful blow to the back of the knee could tear all the leg muscles causing the leg to collapse and severely impair mobility.
- **Shin**: the bone here is very close to the surface of the skin and is unprotected by soft tissue or muscle. Broken skin and bone bruises are the result of a moderate blow. A particularly powerful one could fracture the bone of the shin.
- **Calf**: a powerful blow to the calf causes strong muscle cramps and inhibits mobility.
- **Ankle**: an exposed bone is always a potential target. A well-focused blow could sprain or break the ankle.
- **Instep**: the small bones of the instep can be easily broken by stamping hard upon them.
- **Toes**: like the fingers, these can also be broken relatively easily.

The Body is a Tool

What we have seen up to now is that the body is an instrument. It is no different to a violin, a guitar or the piano. It takes hours of patience and perseverance to fine-tune so that it does exactly what you bid it to. Tae Kwon Do is the means through which this training of the body actually happens.

Apart from being fit, Tae Kwon Do practitioners also seem to be able to move more efficiently. As we have seen already, there are many elements to fitness which Tae Kwon Do instructors tackle in each lesson they teach. The next chapter takes a close look at some of the exercises involved and the benefits that can be derived.

To become effective in fighting, the body has to be used correctly. Here a vertical backfist is demonstrated. Such a move is an unconventional, highly effective, attack against the face, particularly the bridge of the nose. This structurally less powerful punch is extremely fast to execute and can be devastating.

5 Learning the Basics

Most people who decide to make Tae Kwon Do their lifelong goal are usually drawn to it, at the initial stage at least, by its spectacular kicks. Tae Kwon Do, more than any other martial art, has done the most to fix in the minds of the general public the stereotype of a person who is able to fly through the air, kick well above average head height and perform double and triple kicks without having to put the kicking leg down between kicks.

To be able to perform such techniques takes a certain degree of aptitude, a lot of time and true dedication. And yet there is a lot of truth in the saying that 'the journey of a thousand miles begins but with a single step'. There is no martial artist, no matter how accomplished, who has not had to start as an absolute beginner.

Beginning with the basics is always good for form, both for fitness and for the performance of Tae Kwon Do techniques. This chapter is entirely devoted to basic training principles, since fitness, as well as speed and endurance, can only be developed through the development of sound training practices. This happens also to be true for good technique in Tae Kwon Do.

Flexibility

The question most beginners usually ask is how can they increase their flexibility. Unfortunately, there is no magic potion for this. Flexibility helps in the development of speed, it allows the execution of some spectacular kicks and aids in the prevention of injury through hyperextension of the muscles and ligaments.

Everyone has a different degree of natural flexibility. Generally speaking, women and children are more flexible than grown men. This has a lot to do with the flexibility of the hip joints and spinal column but it is also a reflection of the fact that their major muscle groups are not strong and therefore do not need to be held so tightly by the tendons.

There are three general basic body types: endomorph, mesomorph and ectomorph. These will put on muscle in response to exercise at different rates, and are listed in descending order. Most people will be a mixture of two types although there will be some who will fall squarely into one or the other category.

Unless extra work is done by each body type, the order in which they are listed in the paragraph above will also give a fairly accurate reflection of the degree of natural flexibility of each type. Endomorphs tend to be the least flexible. Mesomorphs have an acceptable level of natural flexibility and ectomorphs are the kind of students who may come into a dojang, do minimum warm-up work and then slide into the splits!

In this day and age, very little is ever taken for granted and flexibility should be treated no differently. Just because a person may not have inherited a naturally flexible physique, it does not mean it will be impossible for him or her to look spectacular in the dojang.

Flexibility takes a lot of perseverance (a fine Tae Kwon Do tenet), lots of hard work and a sensible exercise routine.

Determining Your Flexibility Needs

Assessing Your Natural Flexibility

Before beginning exercises designed to make you more flexible it would make sense to determine just how flexible you really are by trying this basic test. Turn the palm of your hand, fingers straight so that you are looking at it. Make sure it forms a straight line with the back of your forearm.

Becoming More Flexible

Despite what was said about there being no secret potion that helps to increase flexibility, there are some dietary changes that will actually make some difference. Cod liver oil food supplements, for example, and fish which is naturally oily (like mackerel or salmon) tend to help the flexibility of the joints thus aiding overall suppleness. A healthy intake of water (currently said to be about 1½ltr each day) also helps the body generate sufficient lubricants in its joints as well as maintaining the natural suppleness of tendons and muscles. It is no accident that all martial arts and sports training manuals advise of the importance of a well-balanced diet that contains sufficient natural oils and fluids. Lifelong proponents of martial arts in China, Japan and Korea swear by a diet which is frugal compared to the average Western diet, as a means of maintaining fitness and aiding longevity.

Now, keep your forearm immobile and bend your wrist towards you so that it forms a right angle. Keep your fingers stiff and straight. Drop your thumb so that its tip points, as much as possible, at the inside of your forearm. Relax the tension on your wrist but maintain the right angle between your palm and your forearm.

With your other hand grab hold of your arm around the base of the wrist and place the ball of your thumb against the ball of the thumb pointing towards your inner forearm.

Held in this position you should now experience a certain degree of strain at the base of your thumb joint and at the base of your wrist. Now apply pressure with your other hand and try to get the tip of the thumb of the bent wrist to get as close as possible to the inside of your forearm.

How Did You Do?

If your thumb touched the inside of your forearm (or even if it hovered less than half an inch away) you are naturally very flexible and you will need to do very little additional flexibility work in order to be able to perform high kicks.

If your thumb bent towards your forearm so that it ran parallel to it (or even pointed towards it) then your flexibility is average. You will need to do some work to increase it but most of your needs should be met by the normal Tae Kwon Do training offered in class.

If your thumb is nowhere near parallel to your forearm (or the tip of the thumb is pointing away) you will need to do some extra work in order to increase and maintain your flexibility.

However, as this is a problem shared by the majority of the population (including some excellent Tae Kwon Do practitioners), there are many exercises designed to aid you in the task.

First, let us look at the different types of stretching that are available, in order to identify the type that will meet your individual requirements.

This kind of exercise helps develop, improve and maintain the flexibility of joints, tendons and spine required for the correct execution of complex kicks. Very few people, however, are able to do it immediately and it will take a tremendous amount of work, commitment and perseverance to achieve. However, as with all forms of stretching, a little, done frequently, will actually result in greater improvements than lengthy sessions on an infrequent basis.

Successful stretching is often the direct result of working on the flexibility of joints, tendons and the spine. A basic exercise which works all three is pictured here. Sit with the body held upright, soles of the feet together and held as close to your body as possible. Hold that position to a slow count of thirty. Then, when your body has become accustomed to the position, grab hold of your ankles, exhale deeply and lower your head towards your feet.

Different Types of Stretching

There are three different types of stretching exercises: ballistic, passive and active.

Ballistic Stretching

Ballistic stretching is found in the type of exercise where the muscles are used to help the tendons stretch in a dynamic, often explosive movement. A good example of a ballistic exercise is when you raise your leg with the knee straight trying to get your thigh to touch your chest. Many of the Tae Kwon Do training techniques are ballistic stretching exercises, so this type of stretching will normally be included during the lesson. Ballistic stretching requires some room, so it is best performed in class. Because the muscles fire violently in order to make the leg fly up in the air, it is also best done only after a thorough warm-up to minimize the chances of injury.

Passive Stretching

Passive stretching utilizes the weight of the body, or the force of gravity, to help increase your flexibility. This is seen most often in films, where the protagonist learns to perform the splits by putting each foot on a chair and balancing in-between. Passive stretching does not require a lot of room, it can be performed at home as well as at the dojang and provided you are sensible, it is probably the type of stretching that offers the least risk of injury. If your body type falls anywhere between an endomorph and a mesomorph, you will need to work on your passive stretching.

Active Stretching

Active stretching is probably the most demanding you can do. It requires strengthening of tendon groups and stabilizing groups of muscles and although it will not increase your passive stretching range and will not help you do the splits, it will help you kick higher and faster with the same effort. Active stretching generally involves pitting one muscle group against another. It can be done with the help of a friend or on your own and it is something all Tae Kwon Do practitioners will work at irrespective of their passive or ballistic flexibility. Because active stretching is time consuming it is not often done in class. Because it needs no warm-up nor requires a great deal of room, it is an ideal stretching exercise for the home.

The Aim of Stretching Exercises

There are, of course, many other stretching exercises besides the ones described in this book. The exercises included here have the twin benefits of being easy to execute and requiring relatively little previous stretching practice. Regular stretching will help to increase your flexibility and will enable you to get the most out of Tae Kwon Do and fulfil your potential as a martial arts practitioner.

Stretching and Abdominal Muscles

Many of the active stretching exercises also help increase the strength of the muscles of the lower abdominal wall, the oblique abdominal muscles and the muscles of the lower back which anchor the latissimus dorsi to the bones near the base of the spine. Because the abdominal muscles as a whole are utilized for the performance of a great many different exercises, stronger oblique abdominals should help you execute a great many other Tae Kwon Do techniques. They also aid in the achievement and maintenance of a better overall posture.

Active Stretching Exercises

If you are naturally flexible, either because you have done a lot of flexibility work in the past or because you happen to be the right body type, then there may be no need to work on passive flexibility, and ballistic work will be included in the class. However, all those who study Tae Kwon Do will need to work on their active flexibility.

Working on Your Own: Basic Stretching

If you work alone you will need a stopwatch to keep track of time and the help of the back of a chair or other stabilizing object.

Stand up straight with both feet together and feet parallel. Now slowly raise one foot off the ground sideways, knee straight, and with the raised foot held in a position parallel to the standing foot. It is important that your trunk is as upright as possible. The temptation here is to raise the foot as high as possible and to drop the trunk so that your head aims towards the floor. The moment you do this, however, the muscles of the lower back and the oblique abdominal muscles relax, destroying half the work you are trying to achieve. So, remember, body held high and leg raised to waist height or just a little higher.

Hold this pose for three minutes if possible. If you cannot hold the pose for that length of time, make a note of how long you actually held it for before you had to lower the leg and try and work towards the magic three minute mark.

Repeat the pose for the other leg. Then, if possible, repeat the pose for both legs.

When you have finished working the legs to the side you can perform the same exercise but with the leg raised, knee straight, to the front. The supporting leg is straight and the toes of the raised foot point towards the ceiling.

Working on Your Own:
Advanced Active Stretching

When you can comfortably reach the three minute mark of the exercises above, you are ready to enter the advanced stage.

As before, extend one leg to the side, feet parallel and body held upright. Now begin circling the whole leg, knee still straight, forming small, rapid circles in the air. Again aim to do this for a full three minutes before you repeat for the other leg.

When you have completed this do the same exercise with the leg extended to the front. Once again, aim for the three minute barrier.

Hamstring stretch: the back of the thigh needs to be stretched regularly to be kept supple. Flexible hamstrings make kicks faster and reduce the risk of injury. The exercise pictured above should be repeated two to three times holding the position on each leg for up to a minute each time. Make sure you exhale slowly as you bend towards the knee.

By working the tendons as the leg moves, these exercises put more pressure on them and thus force them to become stronger more quickly.

Working on Your Own:
Further Exercises

Box splits: even such perfect flexibility as the one pictured here has to start from a position less than perfect. The trick in doing the splits is to allow gravity to work for you. Start by placing your feet as far apart on the floor as you can. Put your hands down next to take your body weight and help you relax the tension on the tendons along your inner thigh. Then hold that position for as long as you can. When you feel you cannot hold it any longer, push your feet out a little further apart and then hold the position for one minute. Slowly relax by bringing your feet back together an inch at a time. Tendons respond more slowly than muscles to physical training so it is important to be patient. Because they respond slowly, however, they are also slow to lose any strength and flexibility they have gained. It is important to try this exercise frequently, but once you have become this flexible you will need relatively little stretching to maintain it.

If you can do the box splits comfortably try this variation. Stretch your arms out in front of you, palms flat on the floor, and reach out as far as you can. Then move your hands towards your feet and lower your body towards the floor until you are lying completely flat. Keep the soles of your feet flat on the floor throughout this exercise. Breathe out as you lower yourself towards the floor. The trick to doing this exercise lies in reaching out as far as you can, then relaxing your lower back and allowing your body weight to slowly pull you down towards the floor. Once again, patience and perseverance are required.

Vertical splits: vertical splits work different tendon groups from those involved in the box splits, and these also need to be worked on. For best results, align the back knee with the front one, put your hands on the floor to balance your body and make sure that your body weight is directly over your hips. Slowly bend your back knee until it touches the floor and then push your front foot as far away from you as you possibly can.

Working With a Partner

If you are fortunate enough to have a partner to help you with your active stretching, you will be able to further accelerate the strengthening process of the tendons. When you work with a partner you do not need a stopwatch but you still need something to support yourself with.

Once again, stand upright with feet parallel. Begin slowly raising your leg as high as you can with the knee straight and your body upright. Your partner puts their hands on your ankle and applies some pressure. The idea is to make the journey of the foot from the floor to its highest position difficult but not impossible. Let your partner know when the pressure applied is too much for you.

Once your leg has reached the highest position possible, begin the reverse journey towards the floor. Your partner now changes grip and begins applying pressure upwards making it hard for you to put your leg down. Repeat two or three times until your leg is tired and repeat on the other leg.

When you have finished with your side leg raises, turn your body and do the same to the front. Once again, your partner should apply some pressure both when you raise your leg and then again when you lower it. By working against pressure on both the way up and the way down, the relevant muscle and tendon groups are worked twice, thus accelerating their strengthening.

The result should be something like what you see in this picture. Keep your body as upright as possible during this exercise, so that you can maintain your centre of gravity over your hips. If it helps, support yourself by holding on to your legs. This helps to put a little more pressure on the legs in order to further stretch your hamstrings.

When you are working with a partner you may find it easier to do the leg raise exercises while lying on the floor. This allows your partner to use his or her weight rather than his strength against your leg and assures a smoother application of pressure during the raising and lowering of the leg. It is also useful if your partner is lighter or not as strong as you are, as your partner's weight can be used to counteract your strength.

Active stretching exercises do not usually take up a lot of time. Small groups of muscles and tendons are worked under quite a high load and fatigue sets in quite quickly. This makes them ideal exercises as part of a daily routine. Remember that the benefits of exercise are always cumulative. Doing active

Stretching is a safe activity which can be performed at any age. Indeed, because there is a direct trade off between strength and flexibility, incorporating stretching into the training routine of younger Tae Kwon Do practitioners is seen as a very positive thing. Increasing flexibility at a young age before full strength is gained helps flexibility to be maintained during adulthood. It also improves overall body stance, helping young adults develop physically more harmonious athletic bodies.

Stretching with a partner is all about communication. You have to be able to tell your partner just how much pressure to exert. The advantage is that your partner is able to help you do stretching exercises that you cannot do on your own. It also becomes a good way to measure progress as you are able to measure yourself against your partner.

For this exercise ask your partner to apply constant pressure on your knees while you relax your legs. Then try raising your knees with your partner still applying pressure against them. After about thirty seconds relax your legs again and allow your partner to apply pressure downwards.

stretching, for example, for ten minutes per day, five days a week, by the end of the week will amount to fifty minutes of exercise which you otherwise would have not had.

Passive Stretching

At its very best, passive stretching can be spectacular. A person who is naturally flexible may be able to drop down into the splits and hold the position for half an hour without any trouble.

Passive stretching relies entirely on the weight of the body and the force of gravity to stretch the tendons on the inside of the thighs so that you can drop into the box splits position and to stretch the hamstrings (the tendons at the back of the thighs) to allow the legs to stretch into the vertical splits position.

Passive stretching nearly always is best done alone. Stretching by nature is a little painful but passive stretching often seems to come down to a mental struggle, where the

mind tries hard to focus elsewhere in order to ignore the pain of tendons being stretched to their maximum limit.

Recovering from Stretching

There is a paradox associated with passive stretching, because the tendons when they are stretched suffer tiny lesions, known as microtears, along their length. The day after a good stretch you will find that your stretching range has been significantly reduced. This is normal. After a hard stretching session allow a day or two of rest for healing to take place before resuming. If you do not stretch excessively but have made stretching part of a regular routine, then you will need to accept that, after a particularly good session, the next day you will have a reduction in your stretching rather than an increase. Over the next few days however, as the tendons heal, you should see an improvement.

Here is an exercise that you can use to stretch your hamstrings. Your partner stands with knees bent and you place your leg on your partner's shoulder, knee straight. Your partner then slowly straightens his or her legs, stretching the back of your thigh in the process. It is important that you keep the knee of the leg being stretched straight at all times. If, initially, you cannot stretch your leg sufficiently for your partner to stand up completely, he or she should stop at a height that is comfortable for you. The key to success in any stretching exercise is time. You need to give your muscles and tendons time to relax and become accustomed to their new, stretched position. When that happens, ask your partner to go a little higher, helping you to stretch more.

The kind of flexibility displayed here is the direct result of cumulative effort over a length of time. It shows that you can always expand your stretching capability provided that you stretch regularly and systematically so that there are no great spans of time between stretching sessions.

It is always best to be thoroughly warmed up before you attempt passive stretching. A quick run beforehand, some kicks, leg raises or any other exercise that will quicken the pulse and get blood flowing rapidly throughout the body is good.

To get into the box splits, stand with your legs as far apart as they will go. Make sure your feet are turned so the toes point to the front. Drop your body from the waist down until your hands touch down and take 50 per cent of your weight on your hands.

Your weight, at this early stage, should be evenly distributed between your legs and hands. Make sure your knees are straight. Hold the position to a slow count of sixty and then slowly slide your feet out another half an inch. Hold it to another slow count of sixty. When you finish the second count, turn your hands so that your fingers now face behind you and place your palms on the floor directly in line with your knee joints. This change in position shifts the weight distribution of your body from your hands and legs to your legs only. Your centre of gravity now should be directly over your hips. Your hands are used to help maintain your balance only.

This means that when you are balancing like this the entire mass of the planet is pulling you down towards its centre. Slowly slide out one foot further away from you. Keep the other where it is. Hold this position until the pain in the inside of your thighs begins to get too much for you. Then slide out a little more and hold to a slow count of sixty.

Relaxing the tendons after stretching is every bit as important as stretching them. After you have finished, do not just flop to the floor. Slowly move your hands until the weight distribution of your body is once again evenly divided between them and your legs.

Then slowly let your body sit back, but keep your feet where they are. Slowly move them together a couple of inches and shake your legs up and down. Move them together a couple more inches and shake your legs rapidly once again. Finally bring your legs all the way in, feet flat on the floor near your hips, knees together. Move your legs in big movements from side to side with your knees, if possible, touching the floor each time.

Such relaxing movements help the tendons recover quickly and stop them from 'snapping' back too fast. This minimizes the possibility of any injury.

Although few people enjoy stretching, it is necessary. However, while stretching, you should always ensure that the pain experienced is the pain of stretching rather than injury. There is a very fine dividing line between the two, which only you will know.

Everyone has a slightly different pain threshold and everyone's body reacts in a slightly different way. It is vitally important that quite early on you tune in to what your body is saying. A little discomfort as a result of stretching tendons to gain flexibility is fine. Agonizing, searing, pain is a warning that things are not going well, and you should always be on the alert for the danger signals.

A variation to the hamstring stretch is provided by the inner thigh stretch seen here. The principle is exactly the same. What is different is that this time you turn your foot sidewise and slowly allow your partner to lift your leg as high as they can. Inner thigh stretches work on the tendons needed for high turning kicks, side kicks and hook kicks. They also help to improve flexibility for the box splits.

The beauty of working with a partner is that you can work in both active and passive stretching. In the exercise seen here, for example, get your partner to push your leg towards your shoulder, while you keep your knee straight. When your leg cannot go any further reverse the direction and push against your partner while they apply enough pressure to make you work but not enough to stop your leg from moving. Then repeat. This way tendons are worked both in a stretched and in a contracted state.

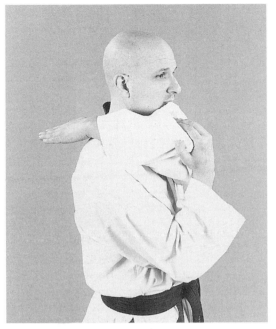

A lot of stretching focuses on the legs and lower body. The shoulder joint, however, is every bit as important and should not be neglected. The exercise shown here helps improve the flexibility of the powerful muscles of the shoulder as well as the tight bundle of tendons holding it.

Another important shoulder stretching exercise is shown here. Place your hand over your shoulder as far down your back as it will reach, then push it further by gripping your elbow with your other hand and applying steady pressure. After thirty seconds change to the other arm. Repeat at least three times.

Ballistic Stretching

Ballistic stretching is less important as part of your home exercise routine as it inevitably takes place when you perform kicks during a class and thus will form part of your weekly lessons in the dojang. It also requires a certain amount of space in which to execute the movements. However, if the inclination exists and you have the available time and space, there are a couple of exercises you can do away from the class.

Vertical Leg Raises
Stand with one leg a little in front of the other. Keeping the knee straight, raise one leg in an upward swing until the thigh touches your chest. Bring it back down in a smooth, controlled motion and then repeat. Do this until you feel your leg getting tired and then change and repeat with the other leg.

Lateral Leg Raises
Stand with trunk upright and feet together. Keeping your feet parallel, swing one leg to the side as high as you can. Try to keep your trunk upright by leaning towards the leg you are raising. Bring the leg down in a smooth, controlled motion and repeat until the leg is tired. Then change to the other leg and repeat.

Other Fitness Benefits

Tae Kwon Do will not just help you with your flexibility. It will also help you with your overall fitness. However, there are as many different ways to measure fitness as there are sports theories regarding fitness.

Some say that the best measure is the ratio of muscle to fat in the body. Others look at endurance, that is, the ability of the muscles to work for a certain length of time without showing signs of fatigue. Another measure is by the VO2 max (the amount of oxygen that the lungs utilize with each breath and then transport to the muscles which need it the most through the blood-stream). The former is often referred to as 'aerobic fitness' and the latter as 'cardiovascular fitness'.

Tae Kwon Do requires the body to move fast and powerfully. During the execution of techniques you will be called upon to use large muscle groups that require a large supply of oxygen, as well as smaller muscle groups. A Tae Kwon Do practitioner must be flexible and must be able to work out for the full length of a lesson. In competition sparring you will need to do these things to your best possible ability.

Tae Kwon Do conditions the body and as such it tackles every aspect of fitness, sometimes all at once.

Conditioning

However often you decide to train in Tae Kwon Do, and to whatever level, the one sure thing is that you will find the need for focused work which helps you get fitter, faster.

While weight training can certainly help in Tae Kwon Do by increasing the strength and power of certain muscle groups, at the initial stages it is not recommended. Weight training usually increases the density and size of the muscles but it also slows the body down and Tae Kwon Do is all about speed.

There are conditioning exercises you can undertake outside the dojang which will be of great benefit when you are performing.

Running

This is good for the strength and endurance of the legs, overall co-ordination as well as stamina and aerobic and cardiovascular capacity. You should try to run as often as you can but avoid running any distance longer than 5km. Physiological studies in the United States have shown that the fibres of the muscles undergo small, structural changes at about the 5km mark which then enable those muscles to keep on running long distances. However, these changes also significantly reduce the short-action fibre of the muscles, which is required in order to enable them to respond quickly. As Tae Kwon Do kicks are all executed in short, concentrated bursts, having short-action fibre in the legs is important.

Sprinting

This is a fantastic exercise from a Tae Kwon Do point of view because it pushes the heart and lungs really hard, it requires the legs to work to their maximum and it hardens other muscle groups of the body, like the abdominal wall, so that maximum power can be generated. Sprint as often as you can and you will soon see the benefits.

Jogging

Different to both running and sprinting, jogging is very good for developing an effective aerobic and cardiovascular system. For the same reason as with running you should, generally speaking, avoid jogging more than 5km. You should always make a point of stretching before and after every run to avoid the tightening up of the muscles and tendons of the legs.

Cycling

This is an excellent way to develop your aerobic and cardiovascular capacity as well as the strength and power of your calves and thighs. Be aware that cycling puts the leg through a very narrow range of movement and as such can be counterproductive when it comes to Tae Kwon Do with its vast range of kicks requiring flexibility and agility. Always stretch carefully after a long cycling session and combine both active and passive stretching in your stretching routine.

Rowing

Again, this is an excellent exercise when it comes to developing the necessary strength and power required as well as the cardiovascular and aerobic fitness. Whether it is done in a gym or out on a lake, rowing certainly puts the body through its paces. Again, stretching is of the utmost importance here. As a rule of thumb any exercise that strengthens the muscles of the body also has the propensity to shorten them. Shorter muscle fibres may be more powerful but they are also more prone to injury and certainly harder to control in the way that Tae Kwon Do training requires. This is why regular stretching before and after any conditioning work leaves the muscles and tendons feeling supple and loose and reduces the incidence of injury.

Theory of Power

Power is the ability of the muscles to do a certain amount of work in the shortest possible time.

A good example of power is to be found in the difference between the strength of body builders who routinely lift weights as heavy

---

'Faster, Fitter, Stronger'

The Tae Kwon Do mantra sounds like something out of the old TV series *The Six Million Dollar Man*. The only difference is that in that series Steve Austin was made able to perform faster, be fitter and more powerful through cybernetic surgery while in Tae Kwon Do you must pay for your gains the old-fashioned way: with sweat. Even at the very earliest stage when students are absolute beginners gains in fitness, speed and power can be made through the repetition of simple exercises. Sitting in the sitting stance, for instance, and practising Tae Kwon Do punches for ten minutes does wonders for limb speed and power, not to mention the strength of the legs and overall fitness.

---

as 20lb (90kg) with their legs and the power of ballet dancers, who would probably struggle to leg-lift their own body weight in the gym, and yet are capable of leaps and bounds which make them seem able to dance on air.

Martial arts is all about power and Tae Kwon Do is no exception to this general rule.

Under a microscope, a single muscle fibre resembles a length of string with beads on it. The beads are the chemical messengers on the muscle which pass on the brain's instructions.

When we think 'run', 'lift', 'kick', 'punch' and 'jump' chemical messengers released by the brain tell the body which muscles should do what and in what order. When a muscle 'fires' or goes to work, it stretches and the beads which act as chemical messengers upon it are pulled further apart. To make a muscle work faster more beads are required along its length and it is at this simple point that all Tae Kwon Do work begins.

There is no better way to build these 'beads' (called neurons) on the muscle than to do repetitive work. A lot of Tae Kwon Do training, traditionally, has been about repetition, starting from basic routines and then advancing to performing complex techniques again and again until the muscles know almost instinctively what is being asked of them and they just do it.

Basic Training

The importance of repetition cannot be over-stressed enough, nor can the benefits to be derived from basic training. Some of the best competition champions, men and women who can effortlessly perform jumping flying kicks, swear by basic training.

The very simple, straightforward kicks and punches which are taught within the first two weeks of training in Tae Kwon Do become the foundation to which everyone sooner or later has to return in order to make further gains.

The next chapter will focus on the kicks of Tae Kwon Do and discuss both how they are executed and, most importantly, how to improve to the point that these kicks become truly explosive.

6   Getting Your Kicks

Of all the techniques employed in Tae Kwon Do, perhaps the most difficult to master are the kicking skills. Successful kicking employs, often under great stress, muscles that are little used in ordinary daily activities.

All students, whether they are beginners or not, must beware of the straining and tearing of muscles and ligaments that may result from kicking techniques performed without proper warm-up and stretching exercises.

A lot of the most spectacular Tae Kwon Do kicks are performed to the head of an opponent, which may appear to be something of a paradox. The head is a naturally hard target. Not only is it a small target when compared to the body but it is also extremely mobile. It can move back, duck down, slip sideways and even bob and weave (as in boxing) making it extremely difficult to pinpoint accurately. So why are many of the Tae Kwon Do kicks focused to the head?

The answer is precisely because it is such a hard target. The head is the furthest target from the feet. If a controlled kick can be delivered accurately and safely to the head of an opponent then it can be delivered with much more devastating effect than an impact on a bigger target lower down the body.

Kicks are one of the most powerful weapons in the human body's natural arsenal. They utilize very powerful muscle groups and they can deliver a blow from a distance much greater than by the hand, thus ensuring a measure of relative personal safety.

Kicks require strength, flexibility, speed and endurance. They utilize, in short, all the skills we have been talking about up to now.

Tae Kwon Do Makes History

Until the 1970s, any martial artist could instantly identify the style from which other martial arts practitioners came simply by their kicks. Karate kickers, for example, always went for long, straight, penetrative kicks with a lot of power behind them, delivered at low targets. Kung Fu practitioners on the other hand always had circular, flashy kicks which required a lot of good balance and more than just good co-ordination in order to work.

Tae Kwon Do went a long way towards changing all this. It was Master Hee Il Cho, one of its earliest exponents in the United States, who first demonstrated to the martial arts world the devastating power and effectiveness of short jumping kicks, by winning one open sparring competition after another in the early 1970s.

It was through Tae Kwon Do, again, that the marriage of short, linear powerful kicks and graceful, arcing kicks came to fruition. Today most styles of martial arts have borrowed freely from each other to the point that the lines of demarcation between each have blurred.

High kicks are used to develop proficient kicking skills and proficient kicking enables a Tae Kwon Do practitioner to deliver explosive power to targets that cannot be reached with the hand.

The Three Types of Kicks

It has often been said that the arm is faster than the leg. Over the same distance and with all things being equal that may be true. Certainly the leg with its powerful leg muscles and greater weight can, by comparison, appear slower. However, with practice and good stretching and conditioning routines the leg can be every bit as fast as the arm and it can deliver far greater power than the arm is ever capable of.

Kicks, essentially, are just another weapon in the arsenal of the Tae Kwon Do practitioner and as such fall into three major categories:

- **Hitting kicks**: these are hard-hitting, penetrating kicks which, when applied in a combat or self-defence situation, are capable of causing internal damage in an opponent.

- **Snapping kicks**: these are speed-oriented kicks. They can be fired off from different directions and their primary purpose is to affect the outer surface of the target area rather than penetrate deeper in.
- **Thrusting kicks**: these are extremely powerful kicks. They are designed to deliver a powerful force to a very small, focused area and as such they are obliterating kicks of the sort usually used in breaking.

Straight Line Kicks and Circular Arc Kicks

For our purposes there are two different kinds of kicks:

- **circular arc kicks** which are made by swinging the leg outside the area occupied by the target in a round or circular motion and then bringing it back into alignment with greater momentum than it would otherwise have been possible (the so-called slingshot effect); and
- **straight line kicks** (or linear kicks) which travel the shortest possible distance between the foot and the target.

When it comes to competition sparring with its fluidly changing situations, there is no way to tell in advance which kick will be the most effective against your opponent. Applying any kick involves split-second timing and the kind of on-the-spot decision which comes only with a lot of practice and experience.

Generally speaking, however, arc kicks, because they travel a greater distance, have the time to gather more momentum and are therefore regarded as being more powerful. In contrast, linear kicks, because they always travel in a straight line, are faster in terms of the time that elapses between the decision to kick and the arrival of the kick on the target.

The chamber position, with the knee held high, leg cocked and ready to fire is the fundamental position from which most Tae Kwon Do kicks are launched. From this position can be launched a turning kick, hook kick, axe kick or a sparring side kick. Apart from the fact that being able to automatically flow into the position prior to kicking is good technique, it has the advantage of keeping a sparring opponent guessing as to what kind of kick you are planning to execute.

All kicks, by definition, are ballistic. The power they generate, however, is a direct function of speed. Fast kicks require strong muscles and supple tendons. If the tendons are not supple enough all the power of the kick will be dissipated in achieving height and it will feel like nothing more than a tap when it hits its target.

A kick is only as effective as the target it is aimed at and each target requires different types of kick. A hook kick, for example (pictured), which is fired from the chamber position, uses the heel of the foot to strike a target. If that target is not a sensitive one such as the head, the kick will not be very effective. Matching the right kick with the right target is often the result of experience as well as skill. This is why sparring is so difficult. Chances have to be seized and decisions made in split seconds.

The Basis of All Kicks

My teaching experience has convinced me that the average novice Tae Kwon Do practitioner is capable of delivering only between 20 to 25 per cent of the power which is available to him or her in Tae Kwon Do kicks.

(left) Kicks are ideal in a self-defence situation when a physically weaker opponent faces a stronger, heavier one. Here we can see the power of a side piercing kick which, if executed without a guard or control, would stop aggressors in their tracks.

The effectiveness of a side kick fired from the chamber position is shown in the sequence below. The kick is fired at a low section of the opponent's body for maximum power, impact and speed.

Power in a kick is a direct function of the kick's speed and the weight of the leg. This is basic physics and it looks like this: weight × speed = power.

This means that the lighter you are, the faster you have to be in your kicking speed in order to deliver the same power as someone heavier than you. Successful kicking, however, is more than just about the weight of the leg and the speed of the kick. It is also a combination of rhythm and timing.

To give an example, suppose in a hypothetical self-defence situation you want to finish an opponent with a single kick. It is possible to deliver, in a kick, 200 or even 300 per cent of your normal kicking power by exploiting your adversary's reaction and momentum to strike at the moment when he or she is coming towards you.

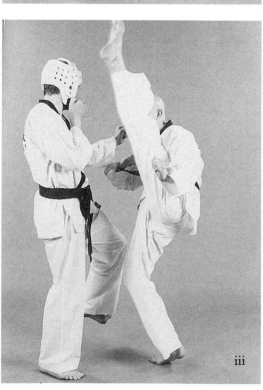

ii

i

iii

iv

The beauty and power of an axe kick is clearly demonstrated in this sequence of photographs. What should be noted is that it also demonstrates the flexibility, tendon strength and muscle strength required to pull it off successfully. All kicks depend on these elements and constant work is required to develop good kicking skills. Again, the criteria of choosing the right kick for the situation apply. An axe kick is of little use for any target other than the head.

This is an example of how the power of a kick is always relative to the situation and the intention of the kicker. Certainly, in competition sparring and in class sparring kicks are executed fast but the aim, always, is to score a point rather than injure an opponent and as such the kicks are always controlled.

The flexibility of the ankle is important when it comes to kicking but then so are the strength of the legs, the flexibility of the hips, the agility of the waist, the elasticity of the hamstrings and the stability of the knee.

All these factors form the basis of all kicks and demonstrate the inherent difficulty in becoming a good kicker. By the same token the reward of suddenly realizing that you can execute good kicks is immeasurable and any sense of achievement gained is more than justified.

The Golden Rules of Kicking

As for most acquired skills, there is best practice even in kicking.

- Be relaxed: tension in the muscles of the kicking leg not only hinders speed but also exhausts the strength of the muscles. It is a physiological fact that tense muscles cannot tense any further. To tense the leg muscles throughout the kicking motion is to waste valuable time and energy. When kicking, the entire leg should be relaxed and it should only tense at the last possible moment prior to impact. This allows the power built up by its journey to the target to be effectively combined with the strength of the muscles to deliver a truly devastating blow. Naturally learning to deliver kicks in this fashion is not something that comes instantly. It takes a lot of practice, perseverance and patience (the 'three Ps').

- Raise the kicking leg high with the knee held bent. This is called the chamber position and it is invaluable to learn to hold the leg like this from as early a stage as possible. Beginners always throw a kick from floor level. This makes it easy to predict its trajectory as the kick will always travel from the floor towards its target in an upward motion. A kick which can be predicted can either be evaded or blocked. Either way, it is not a very successful kick. By holding the leg high off the floor prior to kicking you allow the kick to be delivered in a straight trajectory, parallel to the floor. This makes it a more powerful kick but also it makes it harder to block. When something comes flying at you in a straight line it presents a very small surface area indeed. Blocking a fast kick thrown from the chamber position with the kicking leg held off the ground is akin to stopping a bullet by firing another bullet at it. It does not happen that often! What is more, by holding the leg high in the chamber position prior to firing off the kick you minimize the distance the leg has to travel before it reaches its target and you make the kick faster. You also keep the opponent guessing, as from the chamber position you can fire off any kick, be it a side kick, a turning kick or a hook kick. Finally, from that position a kicker can reach practically any target, be it the opponent's head or his midriff. By keeping an opponent guessing you seize the advantage in a sparring situation and gain control of the sparring match.

- Keep sudden changes in movement and momentum to a minimum. The human body is designed to fight in a forward position and as a result it will instantly react to any change in movement. It is important that prior to a kick you do not change the rhythm of your movements or the momentum of your body. If you were moving keep on moving. If you are still, remain still until the moment you kick. That way you make it harder to telegraph your intentions and you make it more diffi-

cult for your opponent to second guess you.

- Watch your opponent's eyes. This is the giveaway for inexperienced fighters. Their eyes will focus on the part of the body they intend to kick, or conversely they will drop their eyes to concentrate on their opponents' feet, disregarding the fact that an attack may equally well be launched by the arms. By observing what your opponent's eyes are doing you will be able to make better decisions about your own kicks and therefore become a more effective fighter.

It is worth, at this point, to remember that while the kicks that you learn in the dojang are required to display a full range of movement that shows off the development of your own grace, balance and understanding of the principles governing their mechanics, sparring kicks have just one purpose: to get to the target quickly. As such they are stripped to the bone of all finesse and often use 'shortcuts' in their execution.

There is a time and place for everything. Sparring kicks, naturally, need a certain degree of practise. It would be wrong however to practice sparring kicks when doing normal kicking practise in the dojang. Sparring kicks often lead to the formation of 'bad habits' that can make your form look bad. Bad form in the performance of Tae Kwon Do techniques is only a short step behind incorrect application with the accompanying loss of effectiveness, speed and power.

All things being equal, the person with the better technique will always be faster in the execution of a kick.

Single Kicks

Single kicks in Tae Kwon Do can be performed with either the front or back leg.

Aiming Your Kicks

Many people fail to realize that the kicking leg can be aimed just like any other weapon. The trick is always in the knee. When you bring your leg up to kick, your knee should be in a direct line with the target. When the knee of your kicking leg, for example, is pointing at the midriff of your opponent when you extend your leg, your kick will land naturally in that area. Similarly, head kicks always start with the knee directly in line with the head. This also explains the question of power. When the knee goes beyond a target, the delivered kick is also aimed beyond it and is thus a lot more powerful. Conversely, when the knee is in direct line with the target the delivered kick will stop on the surface of the target and no matter how hard or fast it is, it will actually do very little damage.

Generally speaking, front leg kicks are faster but not as powerful as back leg kicks (again because they have a shorter distance to travel). Back leg kicks are more powerful and their reach can often be greater than front leg kicks but they do take longer to get to their intended target. They also require a greater commitment of body weight making it slower for a fighter to recover his balance and react again.

- **Front snap kick**: the fastest, most straight forward kick. Bring the kicking leg off the floor, cock the knee in the chamber position, make sure the toes of your kicking foot are bent back, out of harm's way, and kick with the ball of the foot.
- **Side kick**: once more bring the leg up in the chamber position. Fire off the kick by straightening your kicking leg explosively and by twisting the body slightly to bring your hips in line with the target.

Make sure that at the moment of impact you also straighten your supporting leg. A side kick utilizes the powerful muscles of the lower back as well as the hips and the legs and is, as a result, one of the most powerful linear kicks that can be performed.

- **Axe kick**: this is a variation of the straight leg raise exercise. An axe kick requires you raise your leg to its maximum elevation and then bring it straight down on top of your opponent. Arch your back and push your hips forward during the downward journey of the leg to add more power to its descent and the impact. Apart from good flexibility in the hamstrings the execution of this kick also requires strong tendons at the front part of the leg, where it anchors to the hip.
- **Turning kick** (also known as **roundhouse kick**): bring your leg up high off the ground, knee bent back to the chamber position. From there, using just the power of the thigh and the snap of the knee, whip your leg round to strike the target with either the ball of the foot or the instep.

While the four basic kicks that a student first learns in Tae Kwon Do are described here in simple, pared-down almost, terms it is obvious that there is a lot more to them than just that. The power to be found in any kick is always a combination of the martial artist's strength, flexibility, speed and balance. The ability to kick on the move and to transfer the body weight behind the kick greatly increases the power that can be generated, to the point where even relatively slow kicks acquire tremendous momentum.

There is a certain level of debate as to whether your supporting foot should be flat, to give you the maximum support when you are kicking or whether you should be raised on the ball of the foot thus maximizing your reach and mobility at a potential cost to your balance if you make a mistake. It is worth noting that it was Hee Il Cho who popularized the technique of using only the ball of the supporting foot for balance and certainly his kicks are noted for their speed, snap and power. The best advice is to keep an open mind and experiment to see which technique is most effective for you.

Proficiency in Tae Kwon Do in the dojang and in competition sparring, once the basics have been mastered, is always a choice of personal preference. If you find that a particular technique works for you it would be foolish to abandon it because of perceived doctrine. Similarly, it is unwise to persevere with a movement, which you do not personally find to be effective, simply because someone else recommends it. Tae Kwon Do is a sport of individuals and it is up to you to find your own individual level within it.

The Side Kick

The side kick is such an important kick in Tae Kwon Do that it merits a section of its own. There are many fighters who like to use their side kicks much like boxers use a jab, to stop-check their opponents and to set up other moves without over-committing themselves.

Because the side kick is delivered fastest when the side of your body is presented towards the opponent, it offers the added advantage of minimizing the targets available to your opponent.

The side kick off the leading leg is by far the fastest kick you can do with minimal giveaway body movement. Admittedly, it is not a very powerful kick, but when combined with other kicks such as the spinning hook kick, or the reverse turning kick, or the back kick, it becomes a winning combination that is hard to argue against.

In semi-contact fighting many fighters favour using the side kick almost to the exclusion of many others and it is not uncommon to see fights won entirely on the basis of a fighter hopping or gliding in on one leg and scoring with his side kick.

Because semi-contact sparring does not permit sweeps, such kicking sparring matches can be carried out. For the same reason, Tae Kwon Do fighters feel confident in executing their spectacular high kicks to the head, which make the sport such a pleasure to watch.

Choosing a Leg:
the Importance of Balance

Everyone, regardless of their level of proficiency, will have a favourite kicking leg. For the beginner the favourite leg is also usually the strongest. This is easy to understand but it can also be counterproductive. Effective Tae Kwon Do kicks require good balance and it can be argued that the best balance will be offered by the strongest leg.

Paradoxically, this leaves the weaker leg to do all the kicking. However, apart from the obvious fact that the strength of this leg will gradually be built up during training, it is also important to note that in class and in competition sparring, the actual power delivered by the kick will not be the most important factor.

Sparring in ITF Tae Kwon Do is semi-contact, with the contact areas limited to the front of the upper body and the head. Fast, light, kicks delivered to these areas are difficult and it is more important to ensure that you have the best balance possible when kicking rather than trying to deliver powerful kicks which will make you lose your balance and have you end up on the floor each time.

In order to have good balance and gain the most power out of a kick, the supporting leg is a little bent at the knee, up until the point of impact of the kick when the supporting leg straightens and helps to deliver a little more thrust to the kicking leg.

Double Kicks

Tae Kwon Do is perhaps unique amongst martial arts in that it makes it possible to deliver repeated, rapid blows with the leg. This is achieved through its focus on a modern, upright stance which makes it possible to use the front leg to kick an opponent.

Double kicks, as the name suggests, are kicks where the kicking leg kicks twice with hardly any interval and without touching the floor between kicks.

There are three things which make double kicks possible and they are balance, balance and balance. Balance, however, as we have seen up to now, is the sum result of a number of other factors such as adequate flexibility, a strong supporting leg, timing, focus and tendons that are strong enough to enable the kicking leg to be held in the chamber position.

Although in theory you can launch any double-kick combination, in practice double kicks tend to be either two turning kicks, two side kicks or a side kick and a turning kick. Occasionally there will be the odd turning kick combined with a hook kick but it is not often that such a combination will work in sparring.

Turning kicks work well because they are snappy, strong kicks which are easy to control and that can be very effective against an opponent who refuses to go back after an initial attack and thus leaves himself open to a second attack.

The trick to performing any double kick well lies not just in the execution of the kick itself but in the kicker's ability to cover the ground. No matter how determined an opponent is not to move, after getting kicked once everyone responds by moving a little, even if it is sideways. The success

All kicks, whether single or double, require good balance. It comes down to achieving a good level of muscular control over the body. To help you with your balance, always try and lean in to the kick, rather than away. Make sure the arm of the leg you are kicking with is pointing at your target and your other arm is held close to your chin, rather than trailing towards the floor.

of the second attack (and its power) lies in the fact that a good kicker has a balance that is good enough to allow him to hop or slide half a step (or even a whole step) and thus realign his kicking leg with the target.

Such proficiency does not come easy. In Tae Kwon Do the best kickers are those who from very early on decide to try combinations and difficult kicks, no matter how bad they themselves look while they are attempting them.

Angular Attacks: the Hook Kick

Like a hook thrown by a boxer, the hook kick is an angular attack specifically designed to get round an opponent's defences and deliver a blow. The hook kick is a relatively short kick that will not cover a lot of distance and is thus best reserved for close-quarter kicking.

To work it requires flexibility and, as always, good balance. Again, the leg is held in the chamber position. The foot must be tense and at right angles to the leg, presenting the hard edge of the heel as the striking area.

From the chamber position the leg is swung in an outward arc outside the target and then brought sharply in. The foot is held almost parallel to the floor and the power of the kick comes predominantly from the strength of the thigh and the speed of execution.

The hook kick is perhaps the weakest in terms of the power it can deliver. It is, however, a spectacular kick and it has the added advantage that it can be performed at very close range.

In competition it allows fighters to kick while dropping their upper bodies towards the floor so that they do not offer a target to a counterpunch. Generally speaking angular attacks do not make good self-defence techniques because they take longer to reach the target than the direct, straight kicks and do not pack as much power. They are however very useful kicks, particularly against opponents who like to fight with one leg held cocked in the chamber position. The hook kick also makes an excellent defensive kick against aggressive opponents who like to come in and try to put you under pressure during a sparring match.

Airborne

Sooner or later all Tae Kwon Do students want to try the kicks that most make the sport famous: the flying and jumping kicks. The application of such kicks in modern, fast-paced situations such as self-defence and modern semi-contact sparring continues to be the object of much discussion.

There is no denying, however, that all such kicks visually, perceptually and perhaps even psychologically form part of the essence of all martial arts and Tae Kwon Do especially. The focus, attention and study which has, over the centuries, been devoted to flying and jumping kicks is such that they, quite rightly, form a subdivision of a Tae Kwon Do practitioner's kicking arsenal and are discussed in the next chapter.

7 Taking to the Air

Tae Kwon Do, quite rightly, is known best for its flying kicks. Well-trained Tae Kwon Do practitioners are often capable of executing complicated kicks at targets that are well above their own head height.

Such proficiency never comes easy, and those who are capable of it have often had to work very hard in order to achieve it. Flying kicks look so spectacular that they are often the least questioned kicks in Tae Kwon Do and are, ironically enough, the ones of the most questionable value.

Because of the extreme strain they put on muscles and ligaments and the high degree of accuracy and concentration they require, you need to be thoroughly warmed up before you can attempt them, thus making them of limited use in a self-defence situation.

They are not often used in sparring because the power they generate is such that it is often classed as excessive, although in a slightly modified form there certainly is a place for them within competition.

The first question therefore has to be: why are they practised at all?

Well, simply because they are the epitome of Tae Kwon Do. They allow an individual who is not particularly strong to generate, through a correctly executed flying kick, power which is disproportionate to their weight and physique. They allow, in other words, any well-trained individual to overcome personal limitations and display power, speed and accuracy which many people outside martial arts would class as superhuman.

The Sky's the Limit

Historically, jumping and flying kicks entered Tae Kwon Do as a natural means for foot soldiers to attack cavalry. Because a mounted enemy is less manoeuvrable it was felt that the sacrifice of balance in the total commitment of a jumping or flying kick was justified in the effectiveness of the attack itself and the amount of power it generated against both horse and rider. The effectiveness of such attacks against cavalry was such that in Korea mounted soldiers in the seventh century AD wore thick padded leather armour as protection against Tae Kwon Do kicks, as did their horses.

This is why flying kicks are always going to form part of Tae Kwon Do training. They are one of the requirements of the black belt grading and are always part of the kicking skills on display during Tae Kwon Do demonstrations.

Basic Jumping Kicks

Almost all kicks in Tae Kwon Do can be turned into jumping kicks, but not every kick can be turned into a flying kick.

The main difference between a jumping kick and a flying kick lies in the fact that a jumping kick only requires that the feet

The devastating power of the jumping back kick against mid-level targets is demonstrated by the kick shown above.

front legs change place. Kicks which particularly lend themselves to scissor-motion kicks are the front kick, forty-five degree turning kick (a half-turning kick performed for speed and power) and turning kick. The back leg side kick can be performed as a scissor-motion kick but it takes a disproportionate amount of energy to execute for the energy it delivers. It is a slow kick with few immediate benefits and is thus not used very often.

In competition, sparring scissor-motion kicks are used to break the inertia of an attack and surprise an opponent with an unexpected kick. For this very reason, scissor-motion kicks need to be executed quickly and against low targets (like the midriff of an opponent) rather than high ones.

Two-leg jumping kicks require that the execution of the kick starts with both legs at once. Two-leg jumping kicks, to succeed, need the jump to be higher than scissor-motion kicks. Once again, the front and back leg will change positions and in addition the powerful hip joint will come more into play adding to the overall power of the kick.

Jumping kicks that can be performed with a two-leg jump are: back leg front kick, back leg turning kick, back leg side kick back kick, hook kick, reverse hook kick and reverse turning kick.

It is obvious by now that jumping kicks that require both legs to take off the ground at once lend themselves to a greater variety of kicks. They are also more powerful and more spectacular to perform. At the same time they consume a lot of energy in their execution, and are thus more tiring, and they take longer to reach a target. In competition sparring such kicks are executed only after faster, more direct kicks have set an opponent up, so they are the result of combinations of kicks. Because such kicks run a higher risk of compromising the

clear the ground and is often performed for speed, surprise and power (in competitions and perhaps some self-defence situations) whereas a flying kick, as the name suggests, requires a certain height to be achieved and, possibly, some distance to be covered before the kick can be successfully delivered. Flying kicks are thus best left to demonstrations.

There are two categories of jumping kicks: scissor-motion jumping kicks and two-leg jumping kicks.

Scissor-motion jumping kicks use the initial movement of only one leg to set up the kick and along its execution the back and balance of an attacker they are used in self-defence only as a last resort.

Self-defence situations are a serious matter. They require a speedy resolution and very rarely give anyone the opportunity to warm up beforehand, so a movement which is high-kicking and flashy is usually best left for the dojang.

Flying Kicks

Any kick that is executed with a run up or any kick that covers a certain distance when the kicker is in the air enters the category of flying kicks. Kicks which are particularly effective as flying kicks are the side kick (executed with either the front or back leg) and the back kick.

There is only one reason for performing a flying kick and that is because the kicker wants to focus such an amount of power on a target as to utterly destroy it. Small surprise then, that flying kicks are used in the performance of some of the most spectacular breaking techniques.

So How Are They Done?

Like all kicks, jumping and flying kicks are ruled by a common set of characteristics that need to be addressed for the kicks to be successful. The power for any kick like this comes from the strength of the ankles, calves and thighs as well as the muscles of the lower abdominal wall. Furthermore, a certain amount of flexibility is called for as the rapid switch of legs in mid-air requires the tendons to be flexible enough to respond to the fast flexing of the major leg muscles without running the risk of injury.

- **Scissor-motion front snap kick**: to execute this kick lift your front foot off the floor by about an inch. Keep it where it is and jump over your knee

---

Where's Your Head?

There are two things that impact on the quality of the performance of all jumping, rotating and flying kicks equally and that a lot of people initially get wrong. They are the position of the hips and the position of the head. Whichever kick you are performing the hips should always end up at a 45 degree angle to the target. This allows not only greater reach and flexibility by the kicking leg but, also, generates greater power by bringing into play the powerful short hip-flexor tendons of the pelvic area. Your head must always turn to face the direction of your kick. In a spinning kick this means that the head has to be whipped round quickly to face the target and it is this, that usually allows the body to be rotated fast. Failure to make eye contact with the target prior to the kick leads not only to poorly executed kicks but also missed targets!

---

bringing your back leg into action. Remember to shape your foot so that the kicking leg makes impact with the ball of the foot.

- **Scissor-motion 45 degree turning kick**: this is what is known as a sparring kick in that it is little practised in class and has no formal structure. It is a mixture of a turning kick and a front kick with the instep or the ball of the foot shaped to impact with the target. It is not a particularly powerful kick but it is a fast kick which often surprises an opponent and causes a momentary drop of his or her guard, thus setting your opponent up for the next kick.
- **Scissor-motion turning kick**: in order to execute this kick correctly the kicker must, in mid-air, rotate the hips so that

the back leg can be brought to bear. This gives the kick tremendous power and effectiveness. Unfortunately it also makes it slow and predictable, thus severely limiting its value in the fast-paced world of competition sparring.

- **Back leg jumping front kick**: take off with both legs. In mid-air rotate your hips so that the front and back legs change position. Kick with the back leg as it is being brought to the front. Use this kick against a static target or a static opponent and you will instantly see how powerful it is.
- **Back leg jumping turning kick**: take off with both legs. In mid-air rotate the hips to bring the back leg to bear on the target. Follow through the rotation with your body as you kick. The power of this kick comes from the speed of rotation of the hips in mid-air. This rotation brings the body weight to bear in the kick but requires a certain amount of practice to get right.
- **Back leg jumping side kick**: perhaps one of the most devastating Tae Kwon Do kicks and one that is also suitable for flying kicks. It is executed with the same mid-air hip rotation required by all the other kicks. The difference is that this particular kick allows the entire body weight to be placed directly behind the hip increasing, as a result, the power of the kick by a factor of at least four. This is the kind of kick used against objects that are difficult to break.
- **Jumping hook kick**: this is a kick that can be executed with the front leg as a straightforward jumping kick or the back leg as a reverse jumping kick during which the body rotates 360 degrees. As with all angular kicks both the jumping hook kick and the jumping reverse hook kick are slower to execute than direct kicks. Because they travel a

greater distance however, they tend to be very powerful, particularly when aimed at targets such as the head.

Physics and Physiques

Nowhere does the question of gravity come into focus more sharply than when executing jumping or flying kicks. In both situations the Tae Kwon Do practitioner has to find ways to temporarily defeat gravity. Because the law of gravity is so remorseless, the question of mass (weight) comes into it, hence the importance of physique.

The problem facing anyone who does a jumping or flying kick is not dissimilar to that faced by the NASA Space Shuttle programme, namely how to perfect the thrust to payload ratio for optimum performance. Make the shuttle too heavy, for instance, and the amount of fuel required (which adds to the overall weight) is too much for it to become an effective delivery vehicle.

The same principles holds true for Tae Kwon Do practitioners. Kicking requires strong leg and calf muscles, good strong tendons in the hips, knees and ankles and a certain amount of flexibility in the pelvic area and the bones of the lower back. Training certainly helps to acquire the necessary strength and flexibility as well as the technical dexterity necessary in order to be able to perform the kicks in the first place. However, train with weights and after the initial increase in strength the accompanying increase in muscle mass will negate any gains made. Training, however, is not the only factor. Kickers who are naturally heavier will always find flying and jumping kicks harder and more tiring to execute than their lightweight counterparts.

One of the laws of Newtonian physics states that 'Bodies in motion tend to remain in motion and bodies at rest tend to remain

A jumping hook kick is best executed against a high-section target such as an opponent's head. The trick to all jumping kicks lies in the alignment of the hips after the initial jump and mid-air twist. The kicker in the picture has brought his hips in line with the target exactly as they would be had he been executing the kick from a stationary position. This allows him to whip the leg around, past his body, for maximum power.

at rest': in the latter case this is called inertia and in the former it is called momentum.

With all things being equal however, the success of any jumping or flying kick lies in the ability of the kicker to perform the kick quickly enough so that momentum is not immediately exhausted by gravity. The speed of performance allows the preservation of momentum so that a body moving quickly through the air continues to do so until it reaches its target. It is in this basic principle that the explanation for the almost supernatural performance of flying and jumping kicks is to be found. It also explains why in sparring situations fighters find it easier to be constantly in motion. By moving all the time they reduce their inertia to almost zero and increase their natural momentum, thus minimizing the effort required to execute rapid, powerful techniques.

The power, grace and beauty of Tae Kwon Do is never demonstrated more clearly than in the execution of the flying side kick, seen here performed at head height.

Getting Physical

Tae Kwon Do is a great equalizer. Natural attributes such as height, strength and reach will give some advantages but Tae Kwon Do offers the potential to overcome any perceived physical shortcomings in a sparring match in order to defeat an opponent who is physically superior.

To achieve this you need to develop a good understanding of strategy. To win in competition sparring you must be able to think ahead but you also must be able to recognize the inherent weaknesses and strengths of an opponent. Sparring matches are won by those who can pit their strengths against their opponents' weaknesses and can, in turn, avoid their opponents' strengths.

Strategy in Tae Kwon Do is all about learning how to analyse the situation that you are in. In competition sparring in TKDI you will be matched with opponents who are the same weight as you and the height difference will probably be negligible. However, in team events and in open competitions it is possible that you will find yourself being totally mismatched, facing either an opponent who is much heavier and taller than you or one who is smaller than you are and therefore much faster.

To win in such situations you need sound positional theory, which is the subject of the next chapter.

8   A Sport for All Ages

There are martial arts that require their students to start at an early age. Others have cut-off points past which there is simply no point in enrolling as you are too old to start. Tae Kwon Do is a sport for everybody. Its great mix of kicks, punches, and thrusts, coupled with its great variety of stances, set

By knowing how to attack and what weapons to use, a physically weaker opponent can anticipate and negate an attack from someone who is bigger and stronger.

exercises and patterns makes it ideal regardless of your build, age or sex.

Traditionally the idea of a martial artist has been that of an athletic young man or woman trained to a finely honed physical edge. Tae Kwon Do by definition, however, is more than just about athletic prowess. It is also about cleverly using one's abilities to neutralize a threat. It is about having fun and constantly finding new challenges and it is about using skill instead of strength, experience instead of speed and flexibility instead of power.

It is all these things and more. Being thoroughly modern it is a martial art that uses the latest in scientific fighting techniques to maximize the strength and power of every attack and strengthen every defence. This is where positional theory comes in.

Where You Stand

The very concept of positional theory is based on the fact that if you stand in such a way that you direct the strength of your position against your opponent's centreline it is possible to obtain a 'safe victory'. By 'safe' it is meant that you minimize the degree of risk to which you expose yourself and you make it difficult for your opponent to attack without opening themselves up to a decisive counter-attack.

Positional theory is primarily, then, based with the placement of the body and limbs relative to an opponent at any one time.

Anticipation and correct positioning enables the fighter on the right to deliver a devastating backfist to his opponent. The power of the backfist is augmented by the forward momentum of the opponent as he attempts a punch which never reaches its target.

- does not leave you open to attack without giving you some immediate advantage;
- allows you to maintain a good balance;
- allows you to threaten your opponent more than your opponent threatens you; and
- prepares you to meet any threat from the opponent.

Good positional theory is designed to help overcome such inherent inequalities as those found in situations where a woman has to face a man, a lightweight individual fights against a heavier one, or a slower opponent fights a faster one.

As seen in earlier chapters, the body's major organs lie along an imaginary centreline drawn from the top of the forehead to the centre of the groin. By definition, then, the ideal position to take is one which:

- protects your own centreline against attack;

The Self-Defence Question

The old adage goes that 'the best form of defence is a good offence'. This certainly is sound advice, except that were it to be taken to its natural outcome it would mean that all of us would be fighting half the time and probably more than half of us would be fighting all the time, or at least every time we felt threatened. By far the best course of self-defence is to get out of trouble as quickly as possible. Most of the time this will require a quick turn and a fast sprint.

However, there may still be rare occasions when this may not be possible. It is then that Tae Kwon Do skills can prove invaluable. The objective is still the same: get out of trouble as quickly as possible, but this time by using whatever means of attack or defence are required in order to end the threat of the situation.

It is, of course, far better that a situation like that should never arise. There is simply no compensation for good awareness and appraisal skills. A person who in the middle of the night enters a bar in a questionable area of the town is displaying a poor set of awareness and appraisal skills and may, as a result, end up in trouble.

At its most basic, positional theory is about using one's own personal advantages to defeat an opponent by directing them against his weaknesses. Positional theory is divided into four segments, all of which are relevant to every Tae Kwon Do practitioner in every sparring situation whether within the controlled environment of the dojang, on the sparring mat at competition tournaments or in a self-defence situation. The four segments are: time, space, stance and physique.

Postitional Theory

Time

Time is about seizing the initiative.

If you make the opening attack against an opponent's centreline, while you are attacking your opponent must take the time to defend. The key to seizing the initiative lies in making a threatening attack. An attack which does not threaten your opponent will not force him or her into defending. Instead, he or she will counter-attack in the opening left by your attack. A threatening attack is any attack that masters sufficient force, speed and accuracy to threaten your opponent to the degree that were your attack to be carried to its completion the target would be seriously incapacitated.

In competition sparring, naturally, your attacks are there to elicit a reaction from your opponent, in order to gain you the time necessary to launch your combination of attacks. In self-defence situations, however, attacks will gain you the time necessary to make a decision as to whether to flee (if possible) or escalate the attack until the threat to you is removed.

Space

There are two ways in which any fighter uses space: defensive and offensive. Defensive space is the area within which you can move as you retreat. Boxers, for instance, are extremely adept at minimizing their opponents' defensive space by backing the opponent into a corner against the ropes, from which it is very difficult to retreat. Offensive space is the distance that you can stand from your opponent from which you can launch a threatening attack. This is obviously a question of range, and taller opponents, generally speaking, have an easier time than shorter opponents. In the boxing ring a boxer's reach is very

The effectiveness of Tae Kwon Do's fearsome jumping kicks relies entirely on timing. By timing your attack to slip through your opponent's defences you ensure that it has the desired result. Senior TAGB instructors Kenny Walton (right) and Giannis Peros demonstrate how a turning kick attack can be stopped short by a jumping side kick perfectly timed to hit its target before the turning kick can be fully developed.

A perfect example of the use of space and time is demonstrated here as the defender on the right uses the space around him to retreat sufficiently so he can time his counterattack to coincide with an opponent's punch. This is a classic self-defence scenario which allows the defender to stay out of the attacker's reach.

important, Tae Kwon Do, however, with its fast, high, kicks can neutralize a taller opponent's range by allowing a shorter defender to chose a position from which the legs can be used against the longer reach of the opponent's arms.

Stance

Of all the martial arts, Tae Kwon Do best provides a range of stances that can be used effectively in competition sparring and self-defence as well as training in the dojang.

Stance in positional theory is all about the optimum arrangement of the limbs and the body in order to maximize the opportunity for attack, minimize the chance of an opponent's attack getting through your defence and make sure that at all times you maintain good balance.

Symptoms of a poor stance include improper guard, inefficient, energy-consuming attacking moves and loss of balance.

Physique

Although in Tae Kwon Do we are all equal, in physical terms it may appear that some are more equal than others. Physical advantages can be inherited or improved and they include size, strength, speed, agility, endurance and co-ordination. Tae Kwon Do practitioners who understand positional theory will refrain from launching premature attacks or launching too quickly into their favourite kick combinations. Indeed, the whole point of positional theory is that you use your own natural advantages to create, not to look for, the opportunity to launch an attack.

Irrespective of training, everyone has natural advantages they can use.

• Heavier people are usually also taller.

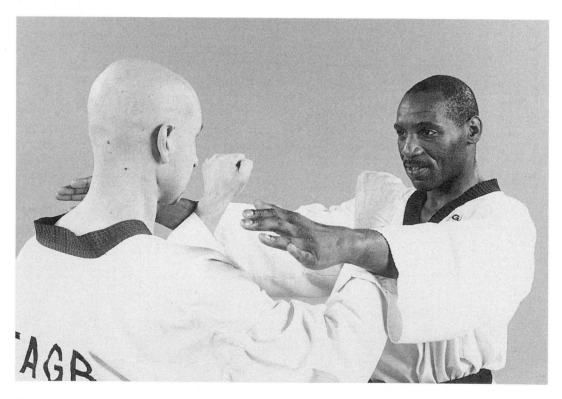

Physique is quite important in self-defence situations where inequalities in strength and size may easily arise. Tae Kwon Do negates some of this inequality through the judicious application of power against the attacker's weaknesses. In the example above a grab for the throat is deflected by applying minimal force on an attacker's arms, near the base of the wrist.

Their attacks have more power behind them, they tend to have the advantage of reach and though they may be slower, their opponents, usually, have to bring the fight to them rather than the other way around.

- Slim, tall people have greater reach, more flexibility and can also get out of trouble quickly by covering the ground faster than their opponents.
- Slim, shorter people usually have a natural advantage of speed as well as natural flexibility. What they lack in strength and reach can be compensated by the fact that they can move very quickly.
- Shorter, heavier people, at face value, seem to have the worst of all worlds. This however is negated if they use their defence well. Being heavier means that their attacks will have more power behind them than, say, someone who is a lot lighter than themselves, and provided that they use their own kicks and punches well, they can usually prove a match for anybody.

Never Too Old

With all we have said so far in mind, a picture is hopefully emerging of Tae Kwon Do being a martial art that has a lot to offer to everybody.

Young children will find that the sport provides them with a challenging, entertaining even, way to master their own bodies and get rid of excess energy. Their natural flexibility and speed will be enhanced while their physical co-ordination will greatly improve.

Children's Tae Kwon Do classes automatically take into account that their bodies are growing and are under a certain degree of strain all the time. The exercises performed are geared towards strengthening them without putting too much physical strain on their bodies and the techniques practised in class help develop streamlined, lithe musculature.

Tae Kwon Do's combination of attack and defence techniques allows each individual to find their own level and improve at a pace that they find comfortable. It is certainly possible for an older person to join a Tae Kwon Do class and reach black belt level provided sufficient training has been undertaken in order to have attained the required level of competence.

Adults find that Tae Kwon Do helps improve their stamina, flexibility, strength and overall sense of balance. Its range of exercises and the training done routinely in the classroom aid in improving co-ordination, burning off excess body fat and the development of lean muscle mass.

Women physiologically cannot easily put on muscle, but the physical benefits for them include a firming up of the upper body musculature (what is known as better muscle tone), enhanced aerobic capacity, better cardiovascular fitness and good lower body strength.

In summary, Tae Kwon Do helps improve:

- flexibility;
- strength;
- agility;
- aerobic fitness; and
- cardiovascular fitness.

It also promotes:

- loss of excess weight;
- muscle toning; and
- improved mental performance.

Of all these benefits, it is probably the last item which most needs clarification.

Mind and Body

As the ancient Greeks discovered so long ago, it is impossible to separate the mind from the body. Training which affects one will almost always have an impact upon the other and Tae Kwon Do with its holistic approach to training addresses the mind as much as the body.

A natural result of regular Tae Kwon Do training is improved circulation, also known as cardiovascular fitness. Cardiovascular fitness is a measure of the capacity of the bloodstream to take oxygen from the lungs and supply it to all of the body's major organs along with other essential nutrients and remove waste products such as lactic acid and carbon dioxide.

Practising Self-Defence

Like most skills, self-defence requires practice. Being a good kicker or being good at competition sparring is never a guarantee that you will be triumphant in a self-defence situation. Practice usually starts with the mind. When you are not training, think about how you could apply what you learn in the dojang to trouble outside it. Sometimes it helps to try out kicks or punches when at home, dressed in ordinary street clothes. Normal clothes are quite restrictive and they can make an enormous amount of difference to the speed with which you can kick or punch.

More often than not, effective self-defence fighting is nothing more than the application of those techniques that are realistically feasible. The thing to remember is that outside the dojang the entire body can be a target and similarly there is no reason why an aggressor will stick to 'clean' fighting without scratching, biting or kicking below the belt.

The brain is one of the body's major organs and any improvement in cardiovascular fitness has an immediate, positive, impact upon its ability to perform. What is more, the concentration required during a Tae Kwon Do lesson in order to correctly perform kicking and punching techniques helps channel the mind to the exclusion of all other distractions. Again, medical studies have shown that this helps significantly in the reduction of stress.

During training the brain releases chemical messengers (known as neurotransmitters) called endorphins. Endorphins have mood-altering properties as well as being natural pain killers seven times more powerful than morphine.

The feeling of well being and a sense of release from care and worry which are the natural after-effects of a good training session are the direct result of the endorphins released by the brain. This is often called a natural 'high' and, depending on the intensity and frequency of your training, can last for up to a day afterwards.

All this is more than enough to provide a reason to take up Tae Kwon Do as a lifelong study, but there is another, which, depending on your own personal viewpoint and personal set of circumstances, can perhaps be more imperative: self-defence.

Tae Kwon Do is a thoroughly modern sport and martial art and as such everything you will learn in the dojang can, if necessary, be applied in a self-defence situation outside it.

Martial Artist Defend Thyself

Self-defence is one of those oxymoronic situations where the people best prepared to deal with it most often never have to. There are a number of reasons why this happens, one of them being awareness. Here we will focus on

In a classic self-defence scenario the defender on the left blocks an overhead attack with an X-block. Such a move is useful because apart from deflecting an attack it also traps the attacking limb or weapon and can therefore give the opportunity to the defender to control the attacker. In the case of trapping the limb, the attack can easily then be terminated by neutralizing the attacker.

practicality, in other words how the stylized techniques of attack and defence and the controlled contact sparring practised in the dojang can be applied in a street fight situation.

This depends entirely on the person who studies Tae Kwon Do. Tae Kwon Do on its own is nothing more than a tool, which will provide a means for channelling tension, releasing stress, promoting health and improving fitness. It will not automatically turn you into a bullet-proof, invincible superman.

The dojang presents itself as a very stylized battleground (for lack of a better word) where attack and defence techniques can be safely practised without running the risk of injury. During training in the dojang Tae Kwon Do practitioners learn responses to attack which are then 'hardwired' in their minds. Hardwired responses are good because they reduce the thinking time required to react to any kind of life-threatening situation and increase the odds for survival. The words 'life-threatening' and 'survival' are used because these are the only situations in which a Tae Kwon Do practitioner would be morally justified in getting involved in a physical confrontation.

The tenets of Tae Kwon Do apart, this is more than just philosophical posturing. Potentially any kind of physical confrontation carries with it the risk of serious injury. Logically there are two types of people you will come across. Those you can defeat without much effort, in which case a fight with them would prove absolutely nothing of value, and those who it is possible could defeat you,

The element of surprise is a powerful weapon in self-defence situations. Being trained and knowing what to do can allow a defender to get the better of an aggressor.

In the pictures here a classic grab and pull attack is successfully countered with a move straight out of Tae Kwon Do patterns.

An arc hand counter to the throat of an attacker would put a stop to most attacks. Every self-defence situation requires the defender to be able to assess its seriousness quickly. An arc hand attack, for instance, is potentially lethal. To execute it when an avenue of escape was open would be to run the risk of prosecution by the law.

niques you have learnt and practised in the dojang are the weapons at your disposal for dealing with the situation. It is not possible to say 'never kick to the head' or 'never punch to the stomach'. Each situation is different and every person is different and what works for one does not necessarily work for another. However, generally speaking, high level attacks, particularly with the feet, in a self-defence scenario, may not be the best policy.

If you ever find yourself in a situation where you may get embroiled in a fight your first response should always be to run. If you cannot run and the person or persons you are dealing with cannot be reasoned with then you will have to fight for your life and fight hard.

Many Tae Kwon Do instructors incorporate self-defence techniques in their lesson in class. Self-defence techniques, as well as reaction time and set responses, are also practised through the execution of one-step sparring which is designed to prepare the Tae Kwon Do student for just such eventuality.

If you ever do find yourself involved in a physical confrontation, fight as if your life depends on it, which in an extreme situation it may do, which is why fighting in the street can never be anything like it is inside the dojang.

Inside the dojang, the behaviour of everyone you fight is governed by a set of rules that are exactly the same as yours. Out in the street the only rule is the primal imperative to come out of the confrontation alive, which is why, sometimes, bare hands and feet may not be enough.

The Armed Response

There is absolutely nothing wrong to respond with whatever comes to hand in self-defence, but before proceeding further it is extremely important to note that the legal point of view

in which case a fight with them would prove absolutely nothing (and risk a great deal).

No one attacks someone else with the intention of doing only a little bit of harm. Granted it is not often that someone attacks you with the express wish to kill you, but an attack is always serious, it can be potentially fatal, and it always calls for a serious response.

This is where Tae Kwon Do training kicks in. The kicks, punches, sidesteps and techis that any self-defence response must match like with like. If, for example, you were punched by a person who was drunk and in response you stabbed him with a knife or used a baseball bat to cause him serious injury then, in the eyes of the law, your response to the perceived threat would be excessive and you could be prosecuted.

If, on the other hand, you were set upon by three or more individuals and you took hold of a handy piece of wood and retaliated so robustly that they were incapacitated, the chances are that the law would be on your side. Indeed, when it comes to escaping with your life the use of anything from a length of hose to stones on the ground is legitimate.

By nature every self-defence situation has to be executed fast and end quickly. Weapons, of whatever sort, give any person a natural advantage over his opponents. Because no one in this modern age travels around carrying a small arsenal with them in case they are ever attacked (and this would, in any case, be illegal), weapons will tend to be everyday objects pressed into a use that their makers had never intended.

This can be anything from household keys held tightly in a fist to provide a rudimentary cutting edge, to an ordinary umbrella which can be used as a truncheon, a handbag which can be swung with force, or the bone handle of a hair comb which makes an excellent stabbing implement.

None of this, of course, need ever come to be used if you are aware of your surroundings and leave threatening situations before they can develop further.

Knowing Before Others Know: Awareness

Awareness is one of those buzzwords that everyone involved in the martial arts scene uses and yet no one can tell you what it is or what you should do in order to develop it.

So let us start from the beginning and ask what exactly is awareness?

Awareness is the ability to quickly analyse your surroundings, appraising each individual or each situation on an individual basis, taking in contextual clues which are almost subliminal in nature and learning to see danger before it escalates to the point where a fight breaks out.

Contrary to popular belief, violence never breaks out at random. Usually there is a lead up to it which to the alert observer is as loud as the hype surrounding a world class heavyweight boxing bout. From certain looks to drunken behaviour, violence is always presaged with little hints and signs that you should pick up and react upon.

Developing awareness is a survival tactic. It takes time and patience. It comes slowly, with perseverance. Tae Kwon Do practitioners are never blind to their surroundings: they always know what people around them are doing.

This is not a call to develop a psychosis or a persecution complex. It is however an admonition to be alert, particularly when you are in surroundings that are unfamiliar to you and may, as a result, potentially, be dangerous.

9 In the Heat of the Battle

Tae Kwon Do was developed with very practical applications in mind. Specifically, it was initially designed as a means of defence against attack by outlaws and marauding bandits and then, subsequently, it was perfected with a view to use in war.

Taken at core value, Tae Kwon Do is nothing more than a means to turn the body into a lethal weapon through training that enables the body to move more efficiently, and teaches effective techniques for attacking other persons and defending against their attacks.

In modern society, however, a few exceptional circumstances notwithstanding, there is very little need for the lethal skills of Tae Kwon Do and the main emphasis is on its application as a recreational vehicle for exploring the physical possibilities of the human body.

There is still a small part of Tae Kwon Do that re-creates, albeit in a much safer environment, a little of its original purpose and use and which requires Tae Kwon Do practitioners to test themselves to the limits of their technical ability.

This is called 'sparring', and more precisely, 'competition sparring'.

A Kind of Combat

Sparring in class is a regular feature of Tae Kwon Do training. It is always carried out in a controlled fashion, under the close supervision of the instructor and while wearing full protective gear. The reason sparring is important is that it develops vital skills which would not be easy to develop otherwise. Some of these are:

*   reflexes;
*   quick thinking;
*   recognition of attacks;
*   familiarization with attack and defence techniques;
*   balance;
*   speed;
*   endurance;
*   timing;
*   focus;
*   co-ordination; and
*   confidence.

While it is true that some of these could be, and indeed are, developed during the normal training in lines during the lesson, it is only within the flux situation of sparring that it is possible to introduce enough variables to really push those taking part to the limit of their abilities.

Because sparring measures, demands and helps to develop so many different skills which lie at the heart of what it means to be a Tae Kwon Do practitioner, it is separated into many different forms. Very early on, students will encounter set sparring and semi-free sparring.

As the name suggests, set sparring is a set of pre-arranged attacking moves which elicit a set of pre-arranged defensive moves. This is a highly artificial situation. Both opponents, for a start, use a controlled, measured

Success in competition sparring is often the result of regular practise in set sparring. This develops the necessary knowledge, reflexes and physical competency required to execute accurate kicks in the highly fluid situation of competition sparring.

pace, their distance is carefully calculated before they start and they both know in advance what to expect and how to react to it. And yet such training routines are invaluable in developing the necessary confidence in the ability to execute more difficult techniques in more challenging situations.

Furthermore, because they are standardized, they provide a readily quantifiable measure of competence in gradings and make it possible to judge the performance of students of widely differing physical attributes and

Set sparring techniques help perfect Tae Kwon Do moves and also generate the level of confidence necessary in order to progress to more ambitious techniques.

ability on a fairly level basis. Set sparring is something every Tae Kwon Do student will have to learn to perform.

Once set sparring has been mastered the student's next step is to practise semi-free sparring. Semi-free sparring is the next logical step in the Tae Kwon Do practitioner's journey towards developing the fighting skills for which the sport is justly famed.

In semi-free sparring the attack moves are standardized (so that the defender knows what to expect) but the defence itself is left open. This allows improvisation on the part of the student and a response which is tailored to individual ability and the set of circumstances imposed by the opponent.

For example: because semi-free and set sparring takes no account of weight and height (or indeed sex) it is possible to have a shorter opponent paired up with a taller one. When it comes to counters some things will be easier to perform and some harder and the snap judgement required in order to decide is close to the skill needed in free fighting, or a self-defence situation outside the dojang.

Seeking Perfection

Every Tae Kwon Do practitioner consciously or subconsciously aims towards the same goal: removing the need to think from the execution of Tae Kwon Do techniques.

Apart from a few physical differences such as muscle density, age and body weight, every person's response time is more or less the same: $1/156$ of a second. That is exactly how long it takes for the message your eyes have seen to be decoded by your brain, be responded to and a command sent to your muscles for them to act on.

Considering the fantastically large number of processes involved in just one single

Developing Sparring Skills

Of all the skills learnt in Tae Kwon Do, the development of a good level of sparring skills probably requires the most commitment in terms of time and effort and, thus, is never too early to start. Practising shadow-sparring (like shadow boxing) moves when at home or before a lesson as a warm-up routine, is a good way of developing and honing physical responses. A five-minute shadow-sparring session, for example, practised at the student's own pace will not only help the body warm up but will also use all those groups of muscles utilized during training in class and will further aid in the development of strength, flexibility and agility.

Set sparring provides a perfectly safe environment for practising self-defence as well as sparring techniques.

reaction to a single stimulus (like, say, blocking an opponent's kick and countering with a punch) this is an incredibly short length of time. Thoughts in the brain are electrical-based and occur at the speed of light. Action in the muscles is chemical-based but still occurs in an incredibly fast time.

Despite this, a reaction time of $1/156$ of a second is too long.

Competition sparring, self-defence and

Practically every age group can benefit from patterns. The moves learnt can be put into practice in real-life scenarios, the muscles are trained, reflexes are sharpened and fitness level is improved.

even normal dojang training require the competent martial artist to flow naturally and easily from one set of techniques to the next without pause, hesitation or ambivalence. Such confidence in movement can only be acquired by practising techniques to the degree that the thinking element in their execution (at a conscious level anyway) is removed.

This is exactly why Tae Kwon Do training (and also many other sports, including ballet and modern dancing) rely on the frequent repetition of techniques in order to develop this non-thinking, almost instinctive approach.

Examined from an Eastern point of view this is akin to Zen. It is the non-thinking state of mind a lot of martial arts masters discuss as the necessary requirement for the attainment of inner harmony. From a purely practical point of view, non-thinking eliminates hesitation on the part of the Tae Kwon Do practitioner and along with it, it also removes of the possibility of uncertainty and fear.

It is these two last elements which normally conspire to foil our attempts to execute something ambitious in Tae Kwon Do, irrespective of whether the setting is the familiar one of the dojang or that of a sports hall during a national competition.

However, the elimination of uncertainty and fear is not always possible. When these two vanish it is often the result of concentration and commitment and when that happens ordinary men and women perform extraordinarily well in gradings, national competitions, Tae Kwon Do demonstrations and Tae Kwon Do lessons.

During those times the feeling experienced by those concerned is that of an intense sense of being. A euphoric high, almost, brought on by the narrow-beamed use of concentration focused on to a single goal. It is the possibility of attaining this state which drives, to varying degrees, every

Tae Kwon Do practitioner from the novice upwards. Like perfection, it is attainable only fleetingly and then only with difficulty. But the very fact that it can be attained makes it worth striving for.

Life on the Mat

Having covered the competition sparring background you would be forgiven for think-

Patterns also help Tae Kwon Do students become aware of the more fundamental dynamics governing the sport. Here, for instance, a double-forearm block is used against a blow that would be too overpowering for anything else. As with everything else in Tae Kwon Do the knowledge of what to apply, when, comes with time and practice.

ing that every Tae Kwon Do practitioner goes down that route. Nothing could be further from the truth. On average only about 10 per cent of Tae Kwon Do students go on to take part regularly in national competitions and competition sparring. This is a reflection, perhaps, of the pressures of modern living which make it difficult to put in the level of commitment in terms of time and effort required by the competition sparring circuit.

Irrespective of whether you decide that competition sparring is something you would like to aim towards, you will usually have the chance to experience it at some level as most Tae Kwon Do clubs hold club events for their members in order to provide some experience in competition.

Competition sparring rules will vary slightly depending on whether you are taking part in WTF or ITF Tae Kwon Do. There are, however, only two major types of sparring:

- point stop; and
- continuous.

Point stop sparring is often used by ITF clubs in the lower belt categories. It is also used in some competitions in higher belts if there are inequalities in the weight divisions. Point stop sparring requires that the sparring match is stopped by the referee after each point is scored and the combatants are returned to their starting marks on the mat. As such, point stop is a fantastic showcase of the speed and technical dexterity of Tae Kwon Do practitioners everywhere. It requires quick thinking and careful planning to set up and gain a point and as sparring matches are a maximum of ninety seconds long the actual time available for getting a 'feel' of an opponent is severely limited.

Point stop competitions are ideal when there is mixed-sex sparring or sparring

The Way to the Top

Sparring competitions are an excellent way of developing fast reflexes and achieving a very good level of fitness. High kicks and jumping kicks are a regular feature of sparring. They are usually performed by students who have invested a great deal of time and effort in their training. What combatants showcase in competitions is not just their ability to punch and kick fast, but also the control they have over their arms and legs. All combatants wear protection and contact is strictly controlled.

between people who belong to different weight divisions, as a lighter opponent can score a point on a heavier or stronger one without worrying about a counter attack. All children's sparring matches are point stop.

Continuous sparring, on the other hand, requires the opponents to spar for ninety seconds without a break. They only stop and part and return to their starting marks on the mat when ordered to do so by the referee and this will happen only if the two combatants are locked in a corner or if the contact is in danger of becoming slightly heavier due to the momentum of the sparring match.

Continuous sparring is a much more realistic sparring match. Even so care is taken to keep contact down to a minimum. Referees are very much aware of their responsibility in this respect. In the UK, TAGB referees receive extensive training on recognizing the dynamics of competition sparring and controlling matches so that any element of risk to the combatants is reduced to the absolute minimum. This has been achieved after many years of consultation and experimentation with clubs, contestants and instructors within the TAGB and the effectiveness of its training is recognized in the fact that TAGB-trained referees are often called to referee in competitions all over the country.

Because of the great degree of physical fitness required to sustain a high level of attack and defence for ninety seconds, continuous sparring demands a higher level of preparation. When practised regularly, in class, it also helps people get fitter faster as it provides an aerobic

The execution of an axe kick in competition, pictured here, requires the focus of mind to recognize what the opponent is doing, take advantage of the opportunity created by their mistakes and execute the winning technique. More often than not winning combinations require a certain amount of setting up. They are rarely the result of luck or blind chance. In order to execute them the Tae Kwon Do practitioner has to be alert, physically fit and fairly experienced. This is why sparring is seen as the nearest thing to a self-defence situation and needs to be practised regularly in class.

and cardiovascular workout and requires the maximum use of agility, speed and flexibility.

Thinking

So where, in all this, comes thinking, or non-thinking? Well, all forms of sparring, whether point stop or continuous, include an element of psychological involvement. Sparring is always against another person, not a machine, and therefore many times success is the direct result of one combatant's ability to focus sufficiently in order to be one step ahead of the opponent in planning and strategy.

Similarly, skilled combatants, who are experienced in competition sparring, will be able to 'read' the sparring situation faster and will restrict and 'guide' their opponents so that they are set up for the use of those techniques which will win the match.

In all this, a certain amount of thinking is involved and the more experienced a combatant is, the less conscious thinking is required and the faster and smoother becomes his or her technique. Practice, like in most other things, brings the reward of a high level of competence, which makes the hardest techniques look easy and the execution of fairly complex strategy look natural.

Sparring Rules and Regulations

It is possible that during a regular lesson in the dojang sparring will take place in an informal basis where each round lasts a lot longer than ninety seconds, there are no referees and students are asked to practise specific techniques. This is sparring for training purposes and, usually, the instructor will be walking among the students making sure that excessive contact does not take place by accident and giving help and advice where necessary.

A hook kick makes swift contact.

A right leg side kick to the high section is put to good use.

Kicks are the essence of Tae Kwon Do.

91

In competition sparring the setting is a lot more formal. In continuous sparring, for instance, there is a referee on the mat with the two combatants (like in boxing) and there are four corner judges who score each successful technique on a point system.

In TKDI sparring competitions points are awarded on the basis of the technique executed:

* kicks to the body score two points;
* kicks to the head score three points; and
* punches score just one point.

In WTF sparring kicks and punches score the same level of points: one point. In addition, in WTF sparring there can be no punches to the head.

TKDI sparring competitions allow punching to the head but the punches have to be controlled, particularly if they are straight punches. No upper cuts are allowed in either WTF or TKDI sparring.

The target zone in both Tae Kwon Do organizations is the body from the waist to the head, but not the back.

Because sparring requires close personal attention and space it can be difficult to practise in class on a regular basis. The problem becomes even more acute if the class is large. Tae Kwon Do instructors are always aware that sparring is tiring and when fatigue sets in mistakes are more likely to happen and injuries due to carelessness are more likely to occur. For that reason much of the sparring training, on a physical level, is done through patterns.

Style and Substance: the Pattern

Patterns are various fundamental movements, most of which represent either attack or defence techniques. These are set to a fixed, logical sequence against one or more imaginary opponents.

Competition sparring in Tae Kwon Do is for everybody. Training for it requires focus pad work for developing strong, accurate kicks and punches. Once again the element of repetition creeps in as techniques, even basic ones, need to be practised again and again until the necessary level of proficiency sets in.

Sparring training is enjoyable and immensely beneficial from a fitness point of view. A great number of Tae Kwon Do students who do not have the time required to travel to competitions nevertheless choose to train competitively simply because of the tangible benefits such training produces.

Patterns allow the frequent practice of techniques such as the arc hand block shown above, which would otherwise not often be practised.

Patterns have a very good basis for their use. Without the discipline imposed by patterns, most students would tend towards practising the techniques that they enjoy and are competent at, to the exclusion of the ones they are not so good at.

Patterns have fundamental moves and challenging combinations in them. As such they force those who practise them to refine their combinations, perfect their fundamental moves and learn the practical basis behind moves which would otherwise look stylized and of little use.

Some of the best Tae Kwon Do fighters in the world are also champions at competitions involving patterns.

Patterns form a logical progression in Tae Kwon Do and it is one of the first things learnt by students, who will begin with a relatively simple pattern. No pattern, however, is easy. They are there to technically challenge the student as well as train muscles to move in a certain way. As such, patterns must be practised as often as possible out-

Although the whole idea of a martial art is to avoid getting hit, blocks are there to protect you when getting out of the way is not a realistic proposition. Some blocks in Tae Kwon Do are more useful in a self-defence situation. Because of this they will be used in class only when self defence is covered. Patterns help bridge the time gaps and keep skills fresh.

side the dojang as well as when in it.

The common theme developing as we progress in our journey through the world of Tae Kwon Do is focus. It is obvious that a certain focusing of the mind is a basic requirement for, and by-product of, Tae Kwon Do training.

It is this focus, as mentioned before, that allows the performance of seemingly super-human tasks in Tae Kwon Do. Nowhere does this become clearer than in the question of breaking, which is the subject of the following chapter.

10   Focusing the Mind

One of the most formidable aspects of martial arts is the ability to destroy inanimate objects made of wood, glass, marble or ice using nothing more than bare hands and feet.

Although breaking, in the West, is primarily associated with Karate, it is a Korean phenomenon developed during the reign of Wang Kon in the tenth century AD when Tae Kwon Do was a regular part of the arsenal of his army. It became obvious that some way was needed to demonstrate the power of his highly skilled troops without sacrificing human lives. The destruction of inanimate objects in regular exhibitions was the method chosen and breaking has formed an integral part of Tae Kwon Do ever since.

Breaking is specifically designed to test the effectiveness of certain Tae Kwon Do techniques and the power they can generate. Because the human body is fairly fragile, breaking is normally practised using specific striking areas of the body. The selection of target to be destroyed is also important. It should be noted that if a break is attempted but is not successful, the power delivered by the movement is not transmitted away through the object but is absorbed by the body and may cause injury.

Materials which are flexible, have strong interlaced grain or fibres in them or have some other means of absorbing the force applied on them are extremely difficult to break, and to attempt to break them is to invite injury.

Normally the best type of material to break is one that is hard but rigid. Brick is an

Why a Target Breaks

The reason a target breaks when it is struck is to be found squarely in the realm of physics. Every target, irrespective of the material from which it is made, displays a tendency to remain stationary. This is called inertia. When a target is struck in the middle of its surface, the force of the blow is transmitted from the hand or foot to the target forcing that section of the target to overcome its inertia and attempt to accelerate. The edges of the target, however, not having been struck, still have inertia which forces them to accelerate at a much slower rate. It is this difference in the rate of acceleration between the middle and the edges of the target which conspires to rip the target apart. You can see now the importance of accuracy in breaking techniques.

excellent example. Ice is another. Wood is the commonest material used in martial arts demonstrations and it can certainly be spectacular, as long as care is exercised to choose a type of wood which is hard, rather than soft.

Breaking Techniques

It is impossible to lay down rules on which techniques can be used in a break. Martial

A powerful side kick goes through a board during a Tae Kwon Do competition. Side kicks are particularly useful when it comes to breaking because they generate a phenomenal amount of power and still allow full visual contact with the target throughout the execution of the technique.

artists are a particularly tenacious lot and there are techniques currently in use at the moment, such as fingertip breaks through one inch boards, which to most ordinary people must seem impossible.

If there is a particular technique which is your favourite and at which you are very competent, it is possible that it can generate sufficient power to perform a break. However, a beginner must always exercise caution. Experienced martial artists have a very good idea about what they can and cannot do. They know enough about the capabilities of their own bodies and the intrinsic qualities of the material they are attempting to break to be able to judge quite accurately whether or not it can be done. Such experience is usually lacking in beginners who, in their enthusiasm at being able to perform a particular technique, may ill-advisedly use it to perform a break.

By far the best breaking techniques are ones that generate a surfeit of power. Usually these tend to be flying kicks, back leg jumping kicks and linear back leg kicks such as front kick and side kick. Reverse or spinning kicks such as the back kick and reverse turning kick are also particularly suitable but they do require a level of technical competence in their performance which usually escapes beginners.

As with all techniques breaking does have a few ground rules which are common to all breaking situations.

- Always judge the distance from your target so that your kick or punch will end up behind it rather than on it.
- Use the power of your hips and lower back, not just your legs or arms, to break through a target.
- Be accurate. To break, a target needs to be struck squarely in the middle. Deviate from this and it is highly likely that the target will not break.
- Maintain eye contact. Use a kick or a punch which will allow you to keep the target in sight throughout the execution of the technique.
- The force of the blow delivered must be roughly at right angles to the surface of the target and travelling with the grain (in the case of wooden boards).
- If you are not certain about how hard the target is, use your strongest technique and choose a kick over a punch.

Going Down the Breaking Path

For the beginner, breaking should begin by performing the technique against a cushioned pad or other soft target. This allows the breaking technique itself to be practised and helps build confidence. This intangible aspect of breaking is also the most important. Targets used in breaking do not move about, they are static. Therefore when they do not break, it is because they have been struck improperly or with insufficient force and that has much to do with the confidence of the person executing the technique. After

all, trying to kick or punch through 1in (25mm) of solid board with nothing more than the naked foot or hand is hardly an everyday task.

That is why it is important to be confident in your ability to deliver the technique accurately and with all the necessary power before you walk up to the target, look at it, concentrate, and then attempt to break it.

Choosing the Technique to Use

Some parts of the body are better suited to breaking than others. The heel of the palm, for example, with its few nerves and hard surface makes an ideal tool for a break. Similarly, the elbow, which is naturally hard, makes breaking easier. Hand breaks are usually performed with the forefist using the front two knuckles or the edge of the palm. The foot also naturally lends itself to delivering devastating strikes which make spectacular breaks.

The thing to remember when you choose with which part of the body to strike the

A palm heel strike is a handy, safe technique for breaking a board. Notice the look of concentration on the face of the person performing the break.

Conditioning allows martial artists to perform almost impossible feats. Here we see a Tae Kwon Do practitioner demonstrate a fingertip break through a one inch board!

target is that the harder you strike, the more stress you will bring to bear onto the striking area. This is why conditioning is very important. If you intend to use regularly your fists to perform breaks, it is a good idea to start conditioning the surface of the fist with which you strike the target.

Conditioning techniques range from striking a softer, less dense target repeatedly to using a cloth-covered heavy stick to strike repeatedly the part of the hand or foot used in breaking. The method chosen will depend entirely on your reasons for wanting to do breaking in the first place. All conditioning techniques involve a certain degree of pain and they all have one aim in common: to form a protective layer of callous over the striking area so that it becomes harder and less sensitive to injury. Note that due to

medical evidence of conditioning techniques possibly causing ill effects, the TAGB and most reputable organizations do not advise any form of regular conditioning beyond what is done in class as part of training.

Breaking Categories

Breaking itself is divided into many different categories.

- Power breaks involve the breaking of many boards, bricks or blocks of ice.
- Air breaks have the target thrown into the air or simply held while it is being struck.
- Jumping breaks usually involve the breaking of a target while jumping over an obstacle.

A hard front fist strike goes through two one inch boards as if they are not even there. This is a classic air-strike with the target loosely held in the air. If the force generated by the strike is not sufficient to create the inequality of forces which are needed to tear the boards apart, or if the strike itself is not accurately placed, the boards will not break. Air strikes are spectacular precisely because the potential for failure is so high. Martial artists train long and hard to develop the necessary speed, accuracy and focus they need in order to be able to get through targets such as the one above.

Tae Kwon Do practitioners with their speed drills in class and their well-developed balance and co-ordination are particularly suited for air breaks. Even then the route to success requires constant practice and refinement of the techniques used.

Notice how the person performing the break has thrown his entire weight forward committing himself totally to the punch. This is a fine example of the level of focus necessary to rid the mind of any hesitancy or doubt which may impair the performance of the air break.

Visualization, as always, plays a big part in this kind of exercise. For the martial artist the board, or target being attempted, is already broken in his mind. All that remains is the need to formally verify the task.

- Blind breaks require that the persons doing the breaking are blindfolded so that they rely on memory and precision of technique to guide them.

All breaks require precision in their execution. The law of inertia is what makes a break possible in the first place. Inertia is a function of mass, and thus if a martial artist can easily break one board, he or she can then go ahead and break two or three. The effort required to impart sufficient energy to three boards to tear themselves apart is not that much more than the effort expanded to break just one board.

Breaking in Class

The Tae Kwon Do student will first come across breaking in class when techniques are practised against cushions or pads held by fellow students. As the technique is perfected and accuracy improves, breaking will move on to a plastic board one inch thick which has a joint in the middle. The resistance of the plastic board is roughly equivalent to that of a one inch wooden board.

The use of the plastic board in class makes sure that during breaking the students do not run the risk of injury through splinters, it keeps costs down and also forces students to be accurate. If the plastic board is not struck directly in the middle and at a 90 degree angle, then it will not break.

Breaking in Competition

Breaking in competition is the ultimate test of power and accuracy. The boards are held in a specially designed 'horse' at a fixed height off the ground. Because of this, competition breaks are more challenging. Not only is the angle of delivery of the force less than 90 degrees to the target, but the person performing the break is under observation.

It is here that it is absolutely necessary to be able to focus the mind to a degree that excludes all outside distractions and focuses on nothing other than the target to be broken.

The Mental Aspect

Tae Kwon Do is an individual sport. You stand or fall by the grace of your own ability and breaking illustrates this starkly. You stand alone, facing a target.

As in any sport your psychological state is all-important. If you have any doubts in your own ability to break through the target, these will surface and will undermine the confidence of your technique and make it difficult for you to succeed.

This is where focus is necessary. What most martial artists do at this stage is use a technique which is now also widely applied in the field of international sports: visualization.

Visualization is also sometimes called 'tunnel vision'. It consists of cutting out by degrees everything that is happening around you until all that remains are you and the target. At this point visualization shifts into the next stage where you need to actually visualize the desired result. You need to see yourself hitting and getting through that target. You need to believe in your own ability to demolish it. And you need to do this over and over again, so that when your turn comes to walk up you will be able to deliver the full power of your potential without any hesitation.

The mental aspect of breaking is a discipline which is used in every part of Tae Kwon Do. Breaking, however, brings it starkly into focus. It is also a link between the safe, cosseted world we live in today and that world of almost 3,000 years ago, when Tae Kwon Do warriors fought for their lives, trusting in their kicking and punching skills to keep them alive.

The Power of a Shout

Of all the elements involved in martial arts the power cry (known in Tae Kwon Do as 'kiai') is probably the one where the greatest air of mystique has built up. Kiai is nothing more than a focused, guttural almost, yell performed during the execution of a Tae Kwon Do technique.

The Western attitude towards self-effacement, which is a facet of modern day living, can make it quite difficult to learn to use the kiai properly.

At its most basic form the kiai is a war cry not unlike those used by our ancestors when charging in battle. Physiological studies have

The power of kiai is demonstrated in this throat-crushing knife-hand strike. The kiai shout allows total commitment of concentration to take place. It would startle and confuse an opponent in a self-defence situation and it allows extra power to be generated by tightening up the abdominal muscles and making it easier to transmit the power generated by the twisting of the hips to the arm executing the technique.

Even simple, straightforward techniques can benefit from the power the kiai shout has to concentrate the mind and body. Here a single punch becomes devastating in its impact thanks to total concentration in execution.

proved that there is a correlation between the kiai and the physiology of the body.

The act of shouting releases certain mood-altering neurotransmitters in the brain which shutdown the neural receptors near the surface of the skin. This has the result of increasing our tolerance to pain. By shutting down these 'extraneous' sources of input the brain is also able to focus more narrowly at the task in hand, whether this is an armed charge against an enemy in combat, or the breaking of a one inch board during a Tae Kwon Do competition.

In unarmed combat, the kiai plays a variety of different roles. The act of yelling while executing a technique expels air from the lungs and tightens up the abdominal muscles. With the abdominal muscles tight the transmission of power becomes easier, making the Tae Kwon Do techniques more powerful.

The kiai is also an extra and often unexpected stimulus to which the opponent must respond. In a self-defence situation an opponent's brain may spend a crucial split second analysing the kiai. Often that split second can make all the difference between life and death, or the success or failure of a technique.

The kiai cry of Tae Kwon Do warriors out of Korea's ancient past was soon exported to Japan where the Samurai adapted it and perfected it into one of the more esoteric arts of martial arts. There are tales of Samurai who were so adept at the use of the kiai that they could use it alone to knock out an opponent.

Medically speaking this is certainly possible. The kiai is a stimulus to which the brain must respond. If the stimulus were to happen at just the right time, with the right degree of surprise and at the right volume then it is certainly feasible that it could overload the brain and result in it temporarily shutting down as a means of protection. Thus unconsciousness could occur.

In practice, attaining such a level of mastery requires a great many years spent analysing human personalities as well as developing the lungs and sternum to produce the volume required for a kiai to make such an impact. This time would perhaps be better spent training Tae Kwon Do combinations. Timing is also important in its application, and aptitude certainly plays a part in the successful execution of the kiai as an offensive technique.

Students often ask me what the kiai cry should be. There is no particular word used in the cry. It is merely a vocalization of energy used to provide focus so it can be anything you feel comfortable with. However it must be stressed that the kiai must be generated from the depths of the stomach and the bottom of the lungs rather than just the larynx. If only the larynx is used, the kiai is no different to the spoken word, and it should be a lot more than that.

In class the Tae Kwon Do instructor will ask students to exercise the kiai with some techniques. However, it will be left up to the student to work on his own kiai. This is just another of the many paths which you'll need to explore in your journey through the world of Tae Kwon Do.

Tae Kwon Do, despite its modern appeal, is an ancient discipline. It has as many facets as there are students in its ranks. It is responsive and adaptable to the needs of today's world and, beyond the discipline required in class, it is never restrictive. It is a guide taking you into a strange world where you will be expected to find yourself. To that end it is forever a road of self-discovery.

May your journey in it be as good as that of those who have travelled before you.

11   Attaining Perfection

I have devoted the better part of my life to the art of Tae Kwon Do and have seen it develop from an esoteric discipline known by few people and regarded favourably by even fewer, to something approaching the status of a national sport with an international following.

In all that time I have reflected at length on the principles and philosophy of martial arts in general and Tae Kwon Do in particular. I have observed the effect of martial arts discipline in the development of young men and women. I have been privileged to have seen the benefits of training in Tae Kwon Do on a great many people and I have, over the years, formed my own thoughts about the philosophy that guides the development of the movement.

It was this which first prompted me to try and encapsulate what it is really like to be a martial artist. What one can reasonably and realistically expect. What it is, after all, to be able to perform at a physical level which leaves most ordinary people dazzled. I also wanted to explore the close links between the development of physical ability and psychological maturity.

I would not go so far as to say that every person who practises martial arts in one form or another automatically becomes a more mature person. However, Tae Kwon Do, like most martial arts, demands a lot more than just a good physique and while there is no denying that physical strength and fitness is an advantage, it is also true that the length of the road it leads you down is limited by the limits of physical ability.

The mind, on the other hand, provides a very different aspect to martial arts training. Stories of extreme courage, sporting events where the underdog has somehow managed to win, people under extreme conditions who have performed extraordinary stunts of physical strength and endurance in order to survive, all point towards the power of the mind.

Martial arts, traditionally, started as a mental discipline. Training required the subjugation of the body to the discipline of the mind, often to extremes which allowed the complete compartmentalization of pain, fear and emotion and turned martial artists into truly terrifying fighting machines.

Delving back in history, this single-minded ability to focus on a given task to the exclusion of all others was what made the Japanese Samurai so feared. Having decided, before entering the battle, that he was already dead, the Samurai had no thoughts of fear, emotion or even personal safety clouding his judgement. As a result he was able to win contests which even today stretch credulity, and come out alive. In a sense this is no different to the modern-day equivalent of elite armed forces like the British SAS who, before embarking on a mission, settle all their affairs.

Indeed, the best strategists of any time, men with many years of experience in armed conflict, who had survived battles which many of their peers had not, who were known by the names of Sun Tzu and Miyamoto Musashi, went on to say that the outcome of any deadly conflict, any conflict whatsoever for that matter, is more often than not decided before a single blow has been exchanged, a single shot fired or a single sword crossed.

What they have pinpointed and what I have come over the years to slowly understand is the same thing: the clarity of one's

It takes years of mental and physical training to control a jumping back kick to the throat without having fatal consequences.

mind, the motivations that drive it, and the emotions that colour it, play a far from insignificant role in the body's ability to perform.

However, you may say that this is self-evident. After all, this book has already discussed the close connection between mind and body, the role of Tae Kwon Do in building confidence and the belief that there simply cannot be 'a sound mind' unless there already exists 'a sound body'. Although these ideas may seem obvious in retrospect, it is important not to lose sight of the basic essence of Tae Kwon Do.

The ability of Tae Kwon Do (or any other martial arts discipline for that matter) to focus the mind so that physical limitations can be overcome is not unique to the sport. Any top level sports person in any sporting discipline will be subject to the same benefits. Martial arts, however, is unique in that it is designed to give this 'gift', for lack of a better word, to every person who applies themselves in the sport, irrespective of the level of competence which they have attained.

The reason for this lies back in the history of the development of martial arts. What is of paramount interest to us today is not the past but the direct benefits to be gained in the modern world.

Along with benefits such as fitness, good health (and they are not always synonymous), flexibility, speed, strength and muscle tone, can be added mental development.

The Battle to Win

If we, today, spent time fighting for our lives, I suspect that many of us would be a great deal more mature than we are now. The fact of our maturity would not just be the direct result of the very real awareness of our own mortality, but also a need to feel every aspect

---

Accomplishing Everything

Honours and riches, distinctions and austerity, fame and profit – these six things produce the impulses of the will. Personal appearance and deportment, the desire of beauty and subtle reasoning, excitement of the breath and cherished thoughts: these six things produce the errors of the mind. Hatred and longings, joy and anger, grief and delight: these six things are the entanglements of virtue. Refusals and reproachments, receiving and giving, knowledge and ability: these six things obstruct the way of the sagely minded person. When these four conditions, with their six causes each, do not agitate the breast, the mind is correct. Being correct, it is still. Being still it is lucid. Being lucid, it is free from preoccupation. Being free from preoccupation it is in a state of inaction, in which it accomplishes everything.

Chuang Tzu

---

of the world around us. We would take nothing for granted. But that is not all. The very fear that we might lose our lives through carelessness would make us careful students of human nature. Out of necessity we would learn to judge other persons with a look, and to ascertain their strengths and weaknesses by the way they walked or held their head or said a casual word. We would read their emotions in their eyes and, like poker players (or warriors) learn that the outcome of a battle had been decided before we even engaged in it.

We do not spend time fighting to save our lives. Most of us, if not all, spend time in offices doing jobs that have little use for the skills one would traditionally develop in the battlefield. In martial arts, however, we are in battle all the time. The primary enemy (and one who never really goes away) is ourselves. Physical fear, weaknesses, physical limitations, all these are elements that every martial artist has fought against from the very first day.

These are, also, the elements every martial artist fights against every day of their lives. It may sound dramatic, but it is a fact that you cannot hope to be able to physically dominate a confrontation if you have not yet first prevailed over your own body.

It is precisely because martial artists have to defeat the limitations of their bodies that they become such assiduous students of human anatomy, psychology and physiology. It is precisely because they come, eventually, to master them, that they then can speak with authority over how to master the bodies of others: whether this is in training or in sparring.

Chuang Tzu

Chuang Tzu is a Chinese Taoist text attributed to Chuang Chou who lived between 369–286BC. It is the first Chinese work to deal solely with spiritual subjects and it advocates the transcending of the physical world and calls for a union with the Tao. The Tao, in the Oriental belief system is the mysterious and indescribable first principle of the universe. Witty and imaginative, Chuang Tzu is a work of exceptional literary distinction. In China it became the guiding principle of every person engaged in martial arts. Its call to recognize materialism as a tie to the spirit struck a chord with soldiers and mercenaries training to master their bodies and it became the bestseller of its time. Its message, through thousands of years, on how to attain 'perfection' by ridding oneself of faults such as avarice, greed and meanness still strikes a chord today and has formed the basis of the moral code of modern martial arts.

Even at its most basic level Tae Kwon Do is all about the battle to win. To win not for victory's sake, not for public recognition or accolades, but for the simple fact that the victory will form the first step which will then lead to the next confrontation with one's own limitations.

Having endured pain and gained flexibility, for example, the martial artist then needs to focus on speed, strength, agility, strategy... the list goes on and on. It is a constant process. One which no matter how hard one tries, never really ceases. There is, for example, no one who can say that having trained with weights for six months they are now strong enough not to have to lift weights ever again and can focus on some other aspect of fitness.

It is this never-ending aspect, the fact that the horizon always recedes, which makes Tae Kwon Do a journey rather than a destination. In that sense training in martial arts becomes a guide rather than a prescriptive ingredient and allows each person to seek their own path and grow at their own rate.

The battle to win, in Tae Kwon Do, is always a personal one fought at a personal level and it is different for every man, woman and child. What is constant is the fact that each victory, no matter how small, allows the individual to take another step on a road of self discovery and self mastery and it is in this process that lies the ability to achieve a certain degree of maturity and understanding that is not readily available to the practitioners of any other sport.

The Inner Path

It is tempting to try to be prescriptive and to state that in order for a student to achieve the inner equilibrium necessary for progress in martial arts, a precise formula should be followed in an exact manner.

Sadly, this will never work. For a start it is unclear what exactly an 'inner path' is and what constitutes an 'inner equilibrium'. These are buzz words which have been around martial arts for a very long time and, in my opinion, have contributed to clouding the issue to the point of almost total obfuscation.

If we accept that every person is different and we are all making progress of some kind then the so-called 'inner equilibrium' must more closely resemble a state of inner flux. And as for the 'inner path' – well that is just a fancy way of embodying the thought-world of each person which is so individual that to even attempt to be prescriptive here is to court ridicule.

This may sound controversial. After all, the traditional literature of martial arts is liberally sprinkled with references to 'chi' (or 'ki') without ever explaining what it is (or even how you can become good at using it!). It also talks about 'inner peace' and 'stillness of mind' without really expounding in any great detail. The reason, I suspect, for this approach is precisely because these terms, which have so readily been labelled by the popular media in the West, represent something which is so uniquely personal that it is exceedingly hard to express.

This section is headed the 'inner path' precisely because this is where the discipline of Tae Kwon Do will take every student from the moment they enrol in a class and come up against the very real adversary of the limitations of their own body.

This 'inner path' then is little more than the constant mental adjustment that has to take place in order for the Tae Kwon Do practitioner to accommodate his or her own developing abilities.

While this may sound simple in principle, it is anything but easy in practice. The good news is that while, ultimately, responsibility for the inner development

necessary for your journey in Tae Kwon Do rests entirely on your shoulders, there are certain things you can do to make the journey smoother, easier and a little more rewarding.

Recognizing the Horizon

The most famous anecdote in martial arts has to be the one to come out of Bruce Lee's Hollywood dojo. The great man very rarely taught there himself and then only private lessons with celebrities. It was during one such lesson, apparently, with a film executive from Paramount, that Bruce asked the man why he had decided to take up martial arts. 'So I can be like you', he replied, to which Bruce Lee responded: 'That can never happen. I already exist and you are already you.'

The point is that to take up martial arts in order to be someone else is like trying to assume someone else's persona. If it works

Confucius

Confucius was a Chinese political and ethical philosopher and would-be reformer. Failing to find personal success he went on to teach a great many students who became his disciples, re-writing, altering and augmenting his teachings until, by the second century BC, they were the dominant philosophy in China. Confucius advocated government by personal virtue. His writings are full of admonitions on the exercise of self-control and personal development. As such they have played a significant part in the shaping of martial arts philosophy where the only control exercised upon the martial artist comes from his own strongly-developed set of personal values.

at all it is only for a short time and it leaves you with an empty feeling inside, as you have striven hard to achieve a goal but met with only very limited success.

The best reason to take up martial arts is so that you can be you. The very best possible you that you can ever be. Recognizing this fact is the first, very real, step on the famous 'inner journey'. This is why it is important to approach Tae Kwon Do with a very realistic goal in mind. In all my years of experience I have seen a tiny fraction of students who were able to take to it instantly, bounding through the gradings, performing well in competitions and constantly improving their sparring. These were remarkably gifted individuals who had a natural 'knack' for Tae Kwon Do and the sport suited them well.

For the majority of practitioners, however, the journey is made up of little steps. Each of these little steps will be a personal goal. Your goals can be anything from mastering a particular kick, to doing the splits, or learning the definition of a pattern. It really does not matter and the reason why is precisely because the journey that you are taking, although within a class and surrounded by dozens of other students, is truly a personal one.

To achieve a goal – any goal – is momentous. It is also energizing and allows you to gain experience. In fact, it may be argued that the very process that you undergo in order to achieve a particular goal changes you so as to make you better prepared for the achievement of your next goal.

Goal setting, always within a realistic framework which takes into account your own physical ability, circumstances regarding training, and natural talent, is therefore important. To set a goal is akin to recognizing where the horizon lies. Horizons are important not only because they give us a destination to travel towards but also because they form a natural boundary.

> ### The Righteous Person
>
> The person who, in view of gain, thinks of righteousness; who, in view of danger, is prepared to give up their life; and who does not forget an old agreement, however far back it extends – such a person may be reckoned to be complete.
>
> Confucius

It is true, however, that the moment a horizon is reached, another one is found to exist beyond it. Similarly, in Tae Kwon Do, having travelled towards one particular goal, and having achieved it, it is important to, again realistically, set your sights on the next. This is called moving the goalposts and is a technique that all athletes use to better their performance.

Moving the Goalposts

The student who having mastered hook kick, for example, immediately goes on to practise another kick is setting himself up for a very big fall. For every kick mastered in Tae Kwon Do there will always be another one to practise, and to go from one to another in a linear fashion is to fail to understand properly the overlap in mechanics which exists between kicks and the connections between them. What is more, by training in such fashion, you will also fail to tackle effectively the one aspect of Tae Kwon Do that makes it such a devastatingly powerful martial art: kick combinations.

Instructors, in class, will structure a lesson to expose students to as varied a menu of training as possible. It is also true that in a class consisting of twenty or more people the instructor's role is that of a guide or facilitator. An instructor is there to point the way and allow students to find their own pace of development.

This is why it is important to constantly move your personal goalposts in training to take into account new techniques. A student who having mastered one type of kick decides, in his personal training, to set as his goal to perform the same kick 200 times, is running on the spot and getting nowhere fast.

The best training manuals advise moving the goalposts in such a manner that the magnitude of the challenge for the new achievement remains the same as it was before it was achieved. To return to my example of the student who has mastered one kick, having done that he or she could then go and master the combination of that kick with another, or that kick with a punch. If the student persisted on practising the same kick to the exclusion almost of anything else, he or she would, indeed, become very good at it but that would not help the student to become a good martial artist.

Training one technique would be of no use whatsoever when it came to developing better co-ordination, reflexes, balance and – most important of all – understanding of where, when and how that technique should be applied.

Training a combination of techniques, on the other hand, allows a curious thing to happen. There comes a point where one technique merges seamlessly into the next. Students' movements then stop being discreet beats in space and time and acquire an effortless, almost flowing, quality to them.

It is then and only then that students begin to realize how the things they have learnt and all the techniques they have been taught connect together. And with this realization also comes the comprehension of their own inner transformation. Part and parcel of this transformation is finding the level at which they can use their own inner energy.

Inner Energy

No book about martial arts would be complete without casting a look on what exactly is this so called 'inner energy'.

Most manuals refer to it as 'chi' or 'ki' and it is, essentially, a focus of the mind on a particular goal to the extent of excluding all outside distractions and performing a particular task.

The most famous examples of this kind of concentration usually occur during spectacular martial arts breaking demonstrations. It may be argued, however, that sparring is every bit as demanding of such focus and concentration, as is performing a pattern or even training in class during the performance of particularly difficult techniques.

Despite claims to the contrary, there is no prescriptive way, which will work for everyone, of developing this kind of focus. Like most things that have to do with the individual, this is different for each person. By and large this focus does not come until the conscious or self-critical part of the brain has been partially anaesthetized with exercise and repetitive work (whether this is a mantra or a pattern).

It is here, at this point that the link between mind and body, in other words between exercise and inner psychological development, is most pronounced and for good reason. The need to gain complete and total control of the body, the desire to push it to its limits, to make it perform almost like a finely-tuned instrument requires such a fierce degree of concentration that it is almost impossible not to develop a certain amount of focus.

In my experience students who fail to find this also fail to see inside themselves. Unable to make the inner connection they are unable to set personal goals, let alone achieve them, and soon drop out of training. This is a sad truth. It is also inevitable since martial arts, though suitable for a great many people, can hardly be for everyone.

Until the 1980s, the only people taking the concept of ki seriously were martial artists. For the rest of the world, it was part of the folkloric tradition surrounding the subject and as such it was meaningless. In 1980 two distinct developments took place, which were to play a very significant role for the inner energy concept of martial arts.

First, the study of physics in the Western world underwent a paradigm shift which allowed it to look at the physical world through the eyes of Eastern beliefs rather than reductionist Western values. Secondly, Western medicine began to examine oriental practices such as acupuncture and study the energy meridians flowing through the body.

What has emerged is nothing less than earth-shattering. Physicists discovered that the world view of flowing energy forms and impermanent shapes that Eastern advocates had long held to be true, was indeed so and doctors mapped strange energy flows through the human body which ebbed and waned along channels precisely corresponding to the meridians of ancient acupuncture.

The West is slowly coming to accept that the ki of martial arts is a bona fide fact.

Furthermore, rather than some form of mystical, inexplicable energy, it is a finite, traceable energy flow, found naturally in the body. As such it is affected by diet, training and concentration.

It is exactly the same type of concentration that allows a top-level striker to recognize a gap in a team's defences, make his decision and score a goal before anybody else can react.

It is the kind of concentration which was visible on Linford Christie's face when he broke the world record for the 100m sprint and it is the kind of concentration that I have often seen on the faces of my students when they train in class.

The only ingredient required to achieve that kind of concentration is commitment. Armed with commitment your journey in the world of Tae Kwon Do cannot fail but be a rewarding one, at whatever level you choose to exercise it. This chapter has been given a grandiose title because if there is one thing which drives all of us in the martial arts world, it is that vision of perfection being played out in our heads. The vision of the martial artist perfectly attuned to and in total control of his body. It is a vision which, to a greater or lesser extent, drives all who embark on this path.

It is never achieved because, like the infinite, perfection is an unattainable ideal. But to come close, to almost achieve it and to taste the sublime moment when you have almost touched it – that is worth more than a lifetime's work.

A Note from the Author:
The Philosophy of Tae Kwon Do

Having come this far, covered so much ground and looked at subjects that, at first glance, one would not deem as having a direct bearing upon Tae Kwon Do, it must become apparent that the sport offers the rare opportunity of becoming a lifelong practice.

Indeed, it must be obvious that Tae Kwon Do is a lot more than just an energy-efficient way of punching and kicking, and it is much more than a competition sport and a means of self-defence. It is this very fact that it can be different things to different people that allows it to have the broad popular appeal it currently enjoys.

Having reviewed everything I have written on these pages, there is only one thing left for me to add and it is last not so much because it is an afterthought, but because I do not want anyone who decides to take up Tae Kwon Do to do so because of what it means to me. The strength of Tae Kwon Do and, arguably, its very future, will depend on new people bringing in their own ideas and interpretations. Like a language, like society itself, Tae Kwon Do is living and changing, and where it may go or where it might take us all can only be guessed at.

Beyond the personal interpretations that each one of us brings into the sport and beyond the very personal reasons we each decide to take it up for, and the even more personal reasons we decide to make it a way of life, Tae Kwon Do does stand for something. It has a general, ambitious and overall philosophy which rather than being prescrip-tive and restricting to its adherents is instead a guiding principle – a matrix to build upon.

The philosophy of Tae Kwon Do, ambitious and grandiose as it may sound, is to build a more peaceful world. To accomplish this goal Tae Kwon Do begins with the foundation, the building block that is the individual. The Art strives to develop the character, personality, and positive moral and ethical traits in each student. It is upon this 'foundation' of individuals possessing positive attitudes and characteristics that the 'end goal' may be achieved, and then only through the sum of the lifework of all those involved.

Tae Kwon Do strives to develop the positive aspects of an individual's personality: respect, courtesy, goodness, trustworthiness, loyalty, humility, courage, patience, integrity, perseverance, self-control, indomitable spirit and a sense of responsibility to help and respect all forms of life. This takes a great deal of hard training and many do not reach far enough to achieve perfection in all of these aspects. However, it is the physical, mental and spiritual effort that the individual puts forth that develops the positive attributes and image of both the individual and how he or she perceives others and their place in the world around us.

By helping an individual to develop into a well-rounded and responsible person, Tae Kwon Do gains practitioners who can pass to others, through both their teaching and their personal actions, the principles they have learnt through their Tae Kwon Do training. Individuals unite and become a family, families come together and form a community, communities merge and develop into a nation, and nations are what make up our present-day world. In order to help build a more peaceful world, Tae Kwon Do starts with one person at a time. Gradually groups form, dojangs (schools) emerge, organizations develop, until Tae Kwon Do's philosophy has influenced, in a positive way, enough persons, families, communities, and nation, to someday bring about, or at least help bring about a clearer understanding of the world. One less tinged with prejudice, aggression and the desire to wage war.

The task is not easy. Just like the metamorphosis an individual goes through from white belt to black belt, so the transition of the unification of nations united by laws of peace, is a long and hard task. Tae Kwon Do, in a subtle, low-key manner, strives for this unification. Race, creed, and nationality have nothing to do with Tae Kwon Do. They are all one and the same. Tae Kwon Do reaches toward the total development of the individual and the founding of a peaceful world. No matter what colour a person's skin, no matter what his religion, no matter where lie his national boundaries, the goal is similar: peace and perfection. This peace can only be achieved if each person has found peace within himself. Tae Kwon Do reaches toward the cultivation of this inner peace and the development of a well-rounded responsible individual.

The physical aspects of Tae Kwon Do are merely a by-product of Tae Kwon Do. It is the mental and spiritual development of a person that Tae Kwon Do nurtures and helps give birth to. The philosophy of Tae Kwon Do can be attained through the cultivation and maturity of all three aspects of the Art, physical, mental and spiritual, in each individual. Once each individual has developed in themselves these three aspects then their very existence cannot help but lead to a more peaceful world.

Tae Kwon Do is doing its part in building a more peaceful world, I, as an instructor, am doing my best to attain this goal, and you, as a practitioner of the Art of Tae Kwon Do, have begun to set the world on the path of peaceful unification. Our task is not an easy one. We may not see our goal fulfilled in our lifetime, but we are now planting the seeds which will one day take root and blossom into Tae Kwon Do's philosophy, total positive development of each individual and a peaceful world.

Tae Kwon Do is not a religion. It is not a movement. It is not even a creed. It is not meant to be. It is a principle, a thought, a way of life. It is as open-minded as each of us chooses to make it. It is as effective as each of us becomes. It is as positive as each of us can be.

Life without Tae Kwon Do would be that much poorer and the world would be a different place.

Epilogue

My own journey in Tae Kwon Do began a long time ago when martial arts were neither as well known nor as widespread as they are today and Tae Kwon Do was an obscure form of unarmed combat. In the intervening years I have had the opportunity and pleasure to be taught by some of the best exponents of Tae Kwon Do and, in turn, teach some of its brightest stars of today.

I have seen its membership in the UK grow from a small band of followers into an organization whose membership will soon exceed 20,000. In this time Tae Kwon Do has turned from a lethal martial art associated with the necessities of self-defence to a popular sport aimed at those seeking health and fitness.

Competitions have become professionally organized affairs attended by men and women from all over the world.

This is a natural progression which I welcome, even as I revel in the fact that I, along with a small number of people, participated in its beginning. In years to come, without doubt, Tae Kwon Do will continue to progress. Its membership and popularity will continue to increase and its body of learning will continue to develop and adapt as it has to date.

In preparing this book I had the assistance of many people, many of whom have shared my experience of seeing Tae Kwon Do develop. Some have already played an important part in its development in the UK as well as abroad, while others will be very much a part of its future.

Tae Kwon Do's development has been and is a journey of adventure, certainly, and one which has its roots in the distant past. No matter how much Tae Kwon Do changes, or how much its emphasis shifts from its original lethal intent, the fundamental tenets at its core, I am certain, will remain intact.

It is these tenets and their timeless message on personal values which is as applicable today as it was 3,000 years ago, which make it a means of self-perfection. As we head into the twenty-first century we have taken the first of many steps. But that is how all journeys begin.

May yours be full of growth and peace.

D. K. Olive

Appendix:
Oriental Symbolism

Where Does the Yin Yang Symbol Come from?

These two words can possibly be traced back to the Shang and Chou Dynasty (1550BC to 1050BC). However, most scholars credit the 'Yin and Yang' to the Han Dynasty (206BC to AD220). At this time, the Yin Yang school was founded by Tsou Yen. It combines the ancient philosophy of the five elements (wood, fire, earth, metal, water) which it then weaves into a cosmology of cyclical movements. The reciprocity between the two poles forms a cycle of movement – or the meaning of change. In relationship to the elements, wood and fire belong to the yang, and water and metal to yin. Earth belongs to both yin and yang because it assists both. The yin and yang represent opposite poles, *not* good or evil.

One of the first religions to use the Yin and Yang symbol was Confucianism (179 to 104BC). The Shih Ching and the I Ching were the first Confucius classics to feature the Yin and Yang. They are represented by the T'ai Chi, a diagram of an egg in which dark and light stand for yolk and white. It symbolizes the origin of all creation. From the egg was hatched the myth of the first man, P'an Ku. This legend dates back to the Shang and Chou dynasty in China, and states that P'an Ku was born in Chaos resembling a hen's egg. After his birth, 18,000 years later, Chaos opened out and the yang, the pure light elements, separated themselves from the yin, the base elements of the earth. P'an Ku grew until he was tall enough to hold heaven and earth apart and his body became the various parts of the earth.

The two are said to have sprung from the Supreme Ultimate or T'ai Chi, showing the interrelation of the two: for as one increases, the other decreases. In addition, this symbol shows the perfect balance between opposites, or the great forces of the universe. This portrays that there is no 'real' masculine or feminine nature, but that each contains a part of the other. The two are contained in one circle thus showing that both powers are in one cycle. Instead of being held in antagonism, they are held together to show that they are mutually interdependent partners. One cannot exist without the other. Today, this theory of cosmology has become a philosophy, a way of life in which the cycle of becoming and dissolution between the world of nature and human events has melded.

Many religions and or philosophies use the Yin-Yang as their symbol: Confucianism, I Ching and Taoism.

The Tao teaches that 'all life embodies yin and embraces yang' (*Tao Te Ching*, Chapter 42). All life, all existence, forms from these two. This can be called Philosophical Taoism. The yin and yang explain the rhythm of the ebb and flow in nature and man. In addition, it expresses the relationship between being and non-being. Non-being is considered to a higher plane than being because it is the source, or the foundation. From this point of view Yin is valued more than Yang.

In Religious Taoism the concept of the Yin and Yang is again closely related to the five elements and how they correspond to the different forces and centres in the human body. Religious Taoism considers the human body a miniature cosmos unto its own, following the cycles of the yin–yang movement.

Now, in the twenty-first century, the philosophy of T'ai Chi has grown to new proportions. This philosophy could be equated to having a successful life during each day ('early to bed, early to rise'). Today, the yin-yang symbolizes the dynamic balance of our lives in the world. 'In this we are to balance and harmonize, not only with ourselves and others, but also with the universe – balancing the active yin with the contemplative yang' (*Drehler*, 1990). As we begin to find balance in our lives, we become more whole, more complete, and more at peace with ourselves.

To summarize, the *Tao Te Ching*, Chapter 42 states:

The Tao is the One,
From the One come yin and yang;
From these two, creative energy;
From energy, ten thousand things;
The forms of all creation.

All life embodies the yin
And embraces yang,
Through their union
Achieving harmony.

In India the theory of the three elements in the *Chândogya Upanishad* led to the theory of the three forces, the gunas, and to the later theory of five elements. In China, the theory of five elements coexisted early with the theory of two forces: yin and yáng. In the Spring and Autumn Period there was actually a Yin and Yang School. Later its theories were accepted by nearly everyone, but especially by Taoism. The implications of the theory are displayed in the great book of divination, the I Ching, the 'Book of Changes'.

Yin originally meant 'shady, secret, dark, mysterious, cold'. It thus could mean the shaded, north side of a mountain or the shaded, south bank of a river.

Yin and Yang.

Yang in turn meant 'clear, bright, the sun, heat', the opposite of yin and so the lit, south side of a mountain or the lit, north bank of a river.

Attribute: stillness, stopping
Animal: dog
Body: hand
Family: youngest son
Direction: northeast

Ken, Keeping still – Mountain.

From these basic concepts, a complete system of opposites was elaborated. Yin represents everything about the world that is dark, hidden, passive, receptive, yielding, cool, soft, and feminine. Yang represents everything about the world that is illuminated, evident, active, aggressive, controlling, hot, hard, and masculine. Everything in the world can be identified with either yin or yang. Earth is the ultimate yin object. Heaven is the ultimate yang object. Of the two basic Chinese 'Ways', Confucianism is identified with the yang aspect, Taoism with the yin aspect.

Although it is correct to see yin as feminine and yang as masculine, everything in the world is really a mixture of the two, which means that female beings may actually be mostly yang and male beings may actually be mostly yin. Because of that, things that we might expect to be female or male because they clearly represent yin or yang, may turn out to be the opposite instead.

Taoism takes the doctrine of yin and yang, and includes it in its own theory of change. Like Anaximander and Heraclitus, Taoism sees all change as one opposite replacing the other.

The familiar diagram of Yin and Yang flowing into each other, the earliest attested example of which, strangely enough, occurs on a Roman shield illustrated in the fifth century Notitia Dignitatum, also illustrates, with interior dots, the idea that each force contains the seed of the other, so that they do not merely replace each other but actually become each other.

Unlike Heraclitus, Taoism sees change as violent only if the Tao (Dào) is opposed: If Not Doing (Wú Wéi) and No Mind (Wú Xin) are practised, then the Tao guides change in a natural, easy way, making for beauty and life. Since trying to be in control is a yang (or Confucian) attribute, Taoism sees Not Doing (and Taoism itself) on the yin side of things; but since Not Doing does not literally mean doing nothing, Taoism can use the language of passivity and receptivity to mean something that is actually quite active.

That is especially obvious in the use of the term róu (Wade-Giles jou), 'soft, pliant, yielding, gentle'. Róudào, the 'yielding way', is read in Japanese as judô and is the name of a popular martial art. Judo does not look at all yielding or gentle, but it does employ Taoist doctrine in so far as it is not supposed to originate force or an attack but takes the attack of an opponent and uses the attacker's own force against him.

Thus the great economist F.A. Hayek invoked Taoism in the defence of capitalism, a system that does not seem particularly yielding or gentle, but is based on the laissez faire principle that government should 'leave alone' private property and voluntary exchanges and contracts. The free market would thus be the Not Doing of government.

When it comes to the five elements, earth, water and wood are clearly to be associated with yin. Water, the softest and most yielding element, becomes the supreme symbol of yin and the Tao in the Tao Te Ching. Fire (the hottest element) and metal (the hardest) both are associated with yang. Nevertheless, the Blue Dragon that symbolizes wood is a principal symbol of yang, while the White Tiger that symbolizes metal is a principal symbol of yin. This kind of reversal turns up frequently in the I Ching.

The I Ching is based on the principle of a broken line, representing yin, and an unbroken line, representing yang.

During the Shang Dynasty (1523–1028BC), questions that could be answered with a 'yes' or a 'no' were written on tortoise shells. The shells were heated, then doused in water, which caused them to crack. A broken crack was interpreted as a 'no' answer and an unbroken crack was a 'yes'.

The I Ching elaborates on this by grouping the lines into sets of threes (the trigrams) and into sets of sixes (the hexagrams).

Attribute: movement, initiative, action
Animal: dragon
Body: foot
Family: eldest son
Direction: east

Chen, The Arousing – Thunder.

Attribute: danger
Animal: pig
Body: ear
Family: second son
Direction: north

K'an, The Abysmal – Water, Moon, the Deep.

Attributes: strength, creativity
Animal: dragon
Body: mind

Sky

Attribute: docility, receptivity
Animal: ox
Body: belly
Family: mother
Direction: southwest

K'un, The Receptive – Earth.

There are eight trigrams: Among the trigrams it is noteworthy that in all the children, the sex is determined by the odd line, so that the trigrams are predominately the opposite quality from the sex of the child. Also, we expect water to be associated with yin and fire with yang, but water is the second son and fire the second daughter. The other children are associated with such things as we might expect, for example water turns up again in the third daughter as the Lake.

The arrangement of the trigrams around the compass reflects Chinese *geomancy (feng shu)*, in other words the determination of the auspicious or inauspicious situation and orientation of places (cities, temples, houses, or graves). Chinese cities are properly laid out as squares, with gates in the middle of the

Attribute: brightness
Animal: pheasant
Body: eye
Family: second daughter
Direction: south

Li, The Clinging – Sun, Fire.

Attribute: pleasure, joy, attraction
Animal: sheep
Body: mouth
Family: youngest daughter
Direction: west

Tui, The Joyous – Lake, Mist, Marsh.

Attribute: penetration, following
Animal: fowl
Body: thigh
Family: eldest daughter
Direction: southeast

Sun, The Gentle – Wind, Wood.

sides facing due north, east, south and west. The diagonal directions are then regarded as special 'spirit' gates: northwest is the Heaven Gate; southwest the Earth Gate; southeast the Man Gate; and northeast the Demon Gate. The northeast was thus the direction from which malevolent supernatural influences might particularly be expected. The situation of the old Japanese capital city of Kyôto is particularly fortunate. To the northeast is a conspicuous mountain, Mt. Hiei (corresponding to the Mountain trigram), which is crowned with a vast establishment of Buddhist temples to guard the Demon Gate. Later, Tôkyô (originally called Edo) was laid out with temples to the north-

east on rising ground in the Ueno district; but both the ground and the temples are now entirely surrounded and obscured by the sprawl of Tôkyô.

The I Ching (*Yi Jing*) uses the trigrams by combining pairs of them into sixty-four hexagrams. The hexagrams reuse the trigrams by combining pairs of them into sixty-four hexagrams. The hexagrams represent states of affairs, and the I Ching is consulted through the construction of a hexagram to answer the question.

The construction is carried out either through a complicated process of throwing and counting yarrow stalks, or by throwing three coins. The obverse (head) of each coin is worth 3 points (odd numbers are yang), while the reverse (tail) is worth 2 (even numbers are yin). Three coins will therefore add up to either 6, 7, 8, or 9. The numbers 7 and 8 represent 'young' yang and yin, respectively.

Starting from the bottom up, these add a plain yang or a plain yin line.

The numbers 6 and 9, in turn, represent 'old' yin and yang, respectively, and are called 'changing lines'.

This illustrates an important aspect of the theory of yin and yang: because the 'Way of the Tao is Return', yin and yang, when they reach their extremes, actually become their opposites. The 'old' lines therefore change into their opposites, giving us two hexagrams if any changing lines are involved: the first hexagram, representing the current state of affairs; and the second hexagram, after the changes have been made, representing the future state of affairs. Changing lines are usually denoted by writing the symbols shown below for 9 and 6, respectively.

The text of the I Ching describes the significance of each hexagram and also the special meaning to be attached to the presence of any changing lines.

An example of combining two trigrams is shown on the left. It signifies The Creative: Great success benefits the upright and pure.

Glossary of Terms

Tae Kwon Do is so popular the world over that it was felt that it needed the development of a common tongue. This has been achieved through the introduction of Korean terms for each Tae Kwon Do technique, derived from a very traditional form of Korean that is no longer in use.

This assures both that the terms themselves remain immutable and that a Tae Kwon Do practitioner will be able to train and understand commands given in any dojang anywhere in the world. The Korean terms given below have been transliterated so they can be pronounced in the way that they are written. Note that in Korean pronunciation the 'u' is more like that found in the word 'tulip' than in the word 'umbrella'.

Counting

Counting is useful both as a tempo setter in class and as a way of marking the number of techniques executed when training.

One	Hana
Two	Dool
Three	Set
Four	Net
Five	Dasut
Six	Yasut
Seven	Ilgope
Eight	Yardol
Nine	Ahope
Ten	Yaul

Stances

The Korean word for stance is Sogi and this always goes after the name of the stance itself so, for instance, rear foot stance would be Dwit Bal Sogi.

Attention	Charyot
Ready	Junbi
Parallel	Narani
Sitting	Annun
Walking	Gunnun
L-stance	Niunja
Fixed	Gojung
Rear foot	Dwit Bal
Bending	Guburyo
Vertical	Soo Jik
Close	Moa
Low	Nachuo
X-stance	Kyocha
Diagonal	Sasun
One leg	Waebal

Punching

The Korean word for punch is Jurigi and again it comes after the description of the type of punch so that front fist punch is Ap Joomuk Jurigi.

Obverse	So Baro
Reverse	So Bandae
Vertical	Sewo
Side	Yop
Upward	Ollyo
Upset	Dwijibo
Downward	Naeryo
Crescent	Bandal
U-shape	Digutja
Turning	Dollyo
Horizontal	Soopyong
Knuckle fist	Songarak Joomuk
Front	Ap Joomuk

Blocking

The Korean word for block is Makgi and it follows the block itself so that a circular block becomes Dolli Myo Makgi.

Inward moving	Anuro
Outward moving	Bakuro
Low	Bakat Palmok Najunde
Middle	An Palmok Kaunde
Rising	Bakat Palmok Chookyo
Forearm guarding	Palmok Daebi
Knife hand guarding	Sonkal Daebi
Twin forearm	Sang Palmok
Twin knife hand	Sang Sonkal
Circular	Dolli Myo
Pushing	Miro
Waist	Horyo
Hooking	Golcho
Pressing	Noolo
W-shape	San
Upward	Ollyo
Downward	Naeryo
Scooping	Duro
X-fist	Kyocha Joomuk
X-knife hand	Kyocha Sonkal
Double forearm	Doo Palmuk
U-Shape	Mongdungi
Checking	Momchau
Release from grab	Japp Yosul Tae

Foot Techniques

The Korean word for kick is Chagi. Given the emphasis Tae Kwon Do places on kicking techniques there are several, distinct, recognizable varieties.

Front kick	Ap Cha Busugi
Side kick	Yop Chagi
Turning kick	Dollyo Chagi
Back piercing kick	Dwitja Jurigi
Downward kick	Naeryo Chagi
Rising kick	Olligi
Reverse turning kick	Bandae Dollyo Chagi
Reverse hook kick	Bandae Dollyo Goro Chagi
Crescent kick	Bandal Chagi
Checking kick	Cha Mom Chagi
Hook kick	Golcho Chagi
Sweeping kick	Goro Chagi
Twisting kick	Bituro Chagi
Front pushing kick	Ap Cha Milgi

Other Korean Terms

Kick	Chagi
Strike	Taerigi
Thrust	Tulgi
Three step sparring	Sambo Matsoki
Two step sparring	Ibo Matsoki
One step sparring	Ilbo Matsoki
Three step semi-free	Ban Jayoo Matsoki
Free sparring	Jayoo Matsoki

Useful Contacts

Robert Howe was the first British person to be awarded black belt by Master Ki Ha Rhee, the person who introduced Tae Kwon Do to the U.K. Robert is seen performing a split kick, a very difficult technique to master.

Even as recently as five years ago, finding a suitable Tae Kwon Do club was the result as much of luck as legwork. Times change fast, however, and martial arts clubs have responded to that change. These days, the degree of affiliation between different styles of Tae Kwon Do, the technology of the internet and the popularity of the sport mean that wherever you live, you have a good chance of being able to find a club nearby. It should not take long to locate if you are able to access the wide range of information available on the internet.

In the sections below, useful web addresses and contacts have been given for different countries. Obviously, the information available on the internet changes rapidly, so it is useful to use one of the many search engines available (such as the ones at www. google.co.uk or www.alltheweb.com) to look for new sites.

UK

Tae Kwon Do Association of Great Britain (TAGB): www.taekwondo.co.uk

This is a comprehensive website with cha-trooms and comprehensive listings of instructors throughout the United Kingdom and Northern Ireland.

United Kingdom Global Tae Kwon Do (UKGT): www.bctkd.freeserve.co.uk

This is the website of the local Bradwell Common Tae Kwon Do club but it provides information and links to other sites, events and other clubs as well as a handy map to the headquarters of the UKTD.

TAGB Times
The Tae Kwon Do Association of Great Britain produces a bi-monthly glossy magazine called *TAGB Times*. The magazine focuses on Tae Kwon Do news, developments, personalities and events, and also covers training tips, history and new training methods.

The magazine is on the net at www.tagbtimes.com. You can visit the website to ask for a free copy of the magazine. You can also reach the magazine through its e-mail, editorial@tagbtimes.com.

Ireland
All Ireland Tae Kwon Do Schools: www.taekwondo.ie

This is a comprehensive listing of all Tae Kwon Do Schools in Ireland along with links to each one, listing of addresses and contact numbers.

Austria
International Tae Kwon Do Federation (ITF): www.itf-taekwondo.com

This website covers events, organizations, affiliated sites and clubs throughout Austria and Germany. It also has a handy guide of links of interest to Tae Kwon Do students.

USA
International Tae Kwon Do Association (ITA): www.itatkd.com

This is an American site with a comprehensive listing of club addresses, links to other clubs and relevant sites, comprehensive information on gradings, ranking and affiliation information. It also provides links to sites that explain the philosophy of Tae Kwon Do, dojang etiquette, Korean patterns and Korean terminology (phonetically) with sounds you can listen to and then practise on your own.

www.home.att.net/~easyblackbelt
An enthusiast's site with smartlinks to patterns, martial arts books, movies and more.

Index